Table of Contents

A Note from the Editor	4
A Note from the Author	5
Screenwriting Basics	7
Screenwriting Concepts	25
Story Craft	37
Characters & Dialogue	71
Completing Your First Draft	91
Evaluating Your Screenplay	107
The Rewriting Phase	117
Marketing Your Screenplay	127
The Working Writer	157
The Writer's Life	167

A Note from the Editor

We all have our favorite movies. Our favorite lines. Our most memorable moments. Do you remember the first time you saw E.T. fly across the moon on Eliot's bicycle? Remember the famous diner scene – thank you, Meg Ryan – from "When Harry Met Sally"?

Movies are an important part of our lives – they ignite emotion and make us think, feel and embrace the emotions we feel. But did you ever stop to think about how the movie actually came to fruition? The screenplay is the foundation of all movies. From the stage direction to the cast and crew, the screenplay binds the movie to the big screen.

Alexis Niki offers novice and expert screenwriters the tips necessary for drafting your screenplay, and gives examples to show future Oscar winners how to carefully complete the process. Using the interviews she conducted from Hollywood power-players, and taking tips from other award-winning screenwriters, Alexis perfects the screenwriting process in this tip book. Take a look at screenplay examples from "Rocky" to "Moonstruck" and learn the best way to format and pitch your screenplay to stars.

Let's all go to the movies!

Melanie Nayer
Editor, LifeTips.com

A Note from the Author

Starting a screenplay is a risk: You may never finish it. Submitting it is a risk: It may be rejected. Seeing it turned into a movie is a risk: The public might hate it. If you never take those risks, however, you'll never reap the rewards.

The merit of my book comes from the very fact that I'm a relative beginner in the business. I'm the rookie whose struggles are still fresh in her mind and whose enthusiasm remains undimmed. These pages don't contain a complete philosophy or method, but practical tips that you can consume. If you're a beginner, this book provides encouragement, motivation, and a wealth of information. If you're more advanced, you'll discover some new angles amongst the usual advice.

This book is the result of the risks I've taken in my journey to become a screenwriter. May it help you learn and prosper as you blaze your own path.

Alexis Niki
Screenwriting Expert Guru

My thanks to: Producers Hal Croasmun, Maggie Soboil, and Harry Waterson; director Randa Haines; entertainment lawyer Judith Merians; script consultant Barb Doyon; DreamAgo president Pascale Rey; and the following writers: Andrew Bennett, Mary V. Dunkerly, Susannah Farrow, Rose Gumarova, Ian Noakes, Lindsay Norgard, Joy Perino, and Jackie Pike for their insights and contributions. Pam Schoenfeld and the short-lived Cast Iron Productions for the initial push. Caroline and Eric Giraud, whose New York home served as my workspace for this project. Pedro de Alcantara, for his contributions, fine editing eye, and unwavering love and support.

Screenwriting Basics

1| The Screenplay as a Blueprint

Screenplays are often compared to blueprints, and for good reason. A blueprint for a house represents an architect's vision. It gives detailed information regarding a building's structure, proportions, and materials, enabling the work crew to see and build what the architect sees. Similarly, a screenplay conveys the screenwriter's vision and helps the reader—and later the film crew—see what the writer sees. In the movie The Hudsucker Proxy (written by Ethan and Joel Coen and Sam Raimi), Tim Robbins plays a country hick intent on becoming a successful executive in 1940s New York. He shows his design for a new invention to anyone who will listen. Unfortunately, his blueprint consists only of a circle drawn on a piece of paper. "You know, for kids!" he announces, with an excited smile on his face. But nobody gets it. The board members of Hudsucker Industries think he's an idiot. They don't realize he's just invented the hula hoop, a craze about to sweep the country. In his mind's eye, the Tim Robbins character had a clear vision, but his skimpy blueprint failed to communicate that vision. The script is your opportunity to communicate your vision. No producer will buy a screenplay if he can't see a movie unfolding in his mind's eye.

2| A Collaborative Art

When you've spent months and even years developing a story, it's not easy to listen to others tell you it needs rewriting. In reality, it takes hundreds of professionals to make a movie. You're working with other creative people, and you have to let them bring their talents and vision to the final product, too.

"Creative friction is necessary," says director Randa Haines (*"Children of a Lesser God", "The Ron Clark Story"*). "It stretches you, it pushes you. It's what enables two people to build something greater than each of them could have done individually."

Rewrites, studio notes, development hell, and actor and director involvement are a fact of a screenwriter's life. How does a writer step out from behind her computer screen and navigate collaboration?

"It's important to know how flexible you are," says Haines. "You need to feel confident that you and the director or producer you're working with are in agreement about the movie you're trying to make. If not, if you're making two different movies, the resulting script will be diluted to nothing."

Your collaborator's suggestions may not always be ideal, but they could potentially reveal underlying problems. It's your job to define these problems and search for creative ways of solving them. As you gain experience, you'll learn which battles are worth waging.

If you choose to argue a particular point, speak your piece with confidence, but don't be insulting or dismissive of other ideas. Stick to the essential points and avoid quarrelling over trivial matters. If you find yourself getting worked up, stop talking and start listening. Take notes, thank everyone for their input, and tell them you'll get back to them with some fresh ideas.

When you look at your notes again in private, you may start to see things from a different perspective. Away from the pressure, you just might come up with some great solutions. Bemoaning the screenwriter's lowly status in Hollywood is never the best use of a writer's time or energy. In the end, the only things you have control over are your attitude and the quality of the work you deliver. If your heart is set on screenwriting, pick your battles and your assignments wisely, keep honing your craft, and work on your team player skills.

3| Character vs. Plot

What's more important in a good script, the characters or the plot? That's like asking which came first, the chicken or the egg. In the best stories, characters and plot are solidly intertwined. Story events force a character to make decisions. And the decisions a character makes influence what happens in the story. They each drive the other. Ideally, your script will have both a riveting plot and three-dimensional characters we can care about. That said, there is a difference between plot-driven and character-driven stories. The question is not so much which is more important, but what's the entry point into the story?

If you're writing a plot-driven story—an action film, a spy story, or a natural disaster movie—you probably have some idea of what is going to happen. The bad guys are going to steal a secret weapon and try to gain world domination. The question quickly turns to character. Who is the hero going to be? Who can stand up to these evil villains? And just how bad are the bad guys? What kind of people would do such a thing? For your plot-driven story to really resonate and become something special, you need compelling characters.

The same holds true if you're writing a character-driven story. "*The Painted Veil*" (novel by W. Somerset Maugham, screenplay by Ron Nyswaner) is about an English couple in a loveless marriage set in the 1920s. The wife is a selfish socialite and the husband a timid doctor. When he finds out she's having an affair, he gives her a choice that will change both of their lives forever: to face the scandal of divorce or follow him into the remote countryside where a cholera epidemic is raging. She chooses to follow him, and thus begins her transformation from spoiled brat to mature woman. The plot was triggered by a character's decision, but the main character's transformation was triggered by the plot. Had these two stayed at home, had nothing happened to shake them out of themselves, there'd be no story.

When you start with character, the questions to ask are, "What can happen to this person to totally transform her? What situations will test her to the core? How can I exploit her worst fear? How can I threaten what's dearest to her?" Focus exclusively on plot, and you'll end up with a formulaic story packed with action but performed by puppet-like characters. Focus exclusively on character, and you'll end up with a rambling, talky, pointless script. Whether your concept is character-driven (*As Good as it Gets*, *Tootsie*) or plot-driven (*Alien*, *Titanic*), remember that the best movies deliver both great plots and amazing characters.

4| A Script Is Not Literature

Novels and stories allow for liberties of pacing not possible in cinema. Scripts have to keep moving. The best screen stories unfold with a sense of rhythm and swing through action, sound, and pictures. Every word on the page should contribute to the images and flow of the story.

The key to writing a good script isn't about the beauty of language, it's about telling a rich story within a limited frame. In striving for brevity, screenwriters drop pronouns and commas and don't always use full sentences. Yet their stories should still have the stuff of literature—the emotion, the drama, the experience—without striving to be literature.

A screenplay can be beautifully written, even poetic, but its beauty lies in a tightly structured story. Poetry is reached in an ideal image rendered by a single word, not through lush descriptions. Writing a good script is hard. It takes the same blood, sweat, and toil as writing anything else—and then some. A novelist may balk at the limitations of the script format, but a good screenwriter will find the tight framework challenging and even liberating. Novelists don't necessarily make good screenwriters and vice versa, though a study of both forms could prove useful to all writers. I suggest you compare a novel with the screenplay of its movie adaptation. You may be amazed at how supremely different they are, even though they represent the same basic material.

5| Passion: Yes! Formula: No!

"In Hollywood, everyone thinks they have to be commercial," says producer Maggie Soboil (Myron's Movie). "That often makes for formulaic writing. I don't want formula. I want a compelling story."

If you hope to make a living as a screenwriter, it's important to be savvy about the market and to understand what kinds of concepts sell. But it's equally important not to become obsessed by the market, because the market is difficult to predict. Don't write something just because you think it will sell. Focus instead on coming up with a fantastic concept that you love, and then telling the best, most heart-felt story you can. Your job is to deliver on the potential of the concept you chose without being formulaic or derivative. Producers are in the story-telling business. They buy and sell great emotional experiences. For that, they need...compelling stories! What they don't need are pale imitations of successful movies or gimmicks—car chases, explosions, cheap sex—that have been thrown in to make the story more "commercial." That's writing by formula, and it isn't interesting to anyone.

Instead, keep digging until you find solutions that are unique and fresh. "When I'm considering a story, I'm looking to get excited," says director Randa Haines. If you're passionate about your concept and are willing to keep searching for ways to tell your story in the most exciting way possible, your passion for your material will be hard to resist.

6| Formatting

A script's format allows busy professionals to find the information they need at a glance. A producer estimating a budget can look at a 110-page script in 12-pt. Courier font and know he's dealing with a 110-minute film. An actor can flip through the script and quickly find his lines. A director can count up the number of night shots needed. The conventions of script formatting make it all possible.

Proper formatting is an absolute must for any serious screenwriter. Sloppy formatting screams "amateur" and will get your script tossed in the reject pile faster than you can say, "But you didn't even read the story!" Screenwriting software, such as Final Draft or Movie Maker, makes the task easier, but you still need to understand the conventions. Below are the bare-bone basics, but if you're writing your very first script you'll need to learn more. One of the best overviews of formatting that I've come across is in chapter two of "Screenplay, Writing the Picture," by Robin U. Russin and William Missouri Downs.

· **Length**: 90-120 pages, but 100-110 is considered ideal.

· **Font**: 12-pt. Courier font.

· **Margins**: Top, bottom, and right margins: 1". Leave a larger (1.5") left margin for binding.

· **Scene Headings** (Slug Lines): No indent, capitalize. Start the slug line with INT. or EXT. to indicate whether the shot is indoors (in a room, a car, or a tent) or outdoors. Give the location: DAVID'S APARTMENT. Type a dash and indicate if it's DAY or NIGHT. Don't specify what time (noon, twighlight, etc.). Example: INT. DAVID'S APARTMENT – DAY

· **Action**: No indent. Action, scenery, and character descriptions go here. Keep blocks of text short (3-5 lines).

· **Character**: Use CAPS for all character headings and the first time a character is introduced. Indent character headings at 3.5."

· **Dialogue**: Directly follows a character heading. Start at 2.5," end at 5.5."

· **Parentheticals**: Avoid using them. It's the actor's job to interpret your lines. But if you must use them: Follow a character's name on the next line. Indicate how the dialogue is delivered: (angry), (nervous). Start at 3" and end at 5.5."

· **Camera Angles and Transitions**: Don't use them. This is the director's job.

· **General**: Single space your script, but double space between scenes. Leave lots of white space on the page by limiting your text and dialogue blocks to 3-5 lines.

· **Paper**: US letter-sized 8.5 x 11 inches, plain white, 3-hole punched.

· **Brads**: Use ACCO No. 5 or 6. Use two brads, not three (on the top and bottom holes).

7| Show, Don't Tell

Movies are visual. Their stories unfold through moving pictures—pictures that show action—with the help of dialogue. This is why scripts are always written in the simple present, as if the film were rolling before our eyes. A novelist has the luxury of entering a character's head and reading his thoughts. A screenwriter doesn't. The old adage "show, don't tell" is never more applicable than in screenwriting. You simply can't write anything that can't be shown on the screen or heard in dialogue.

The mark of a good writer is the ability to draw the reader into the fictional world. For screenwriters, this means finding dramatic and visually interesting ways of externalizing everything which is internal, be it conflict, thoughts, or feelings.

In daily life, we read situations all the time. If we notice a couple at a restaurant eating in strained silence, we look for details. Tight lips, lack of eye contact, wedding rings. We watch for emotional cues and listen for tone of voice so we'll know how to interpret a comment. We make decisions and assumptions based on our interpretations.

Part of the fun of reading a story is having the chance to exercise our innate ability to assess situations and reach conclusions just as we do in real life. It makes us feel we are living the experience rather than standing on the outside looking in. Guide your reader skillfully toward the conclusions you'd like him to reach. Mona is upset is telling. Mona throws the dishes across the room is showing. Robert is a neat freak is telling. Robert folds the end of the toilet paper into a perfect triangle and rolls it on the holder until it is perfectly aligned is showing. As entertainment lawyer Judith Merians put it, "A story is what happens, not what one says happens. A young woman smacks down a package of condoms at the checkout stand in the supermarket. She pays without embarrassment, pockets the package, and then calls her husband on her cell phone to tell him she's working that night. This shows us everything we need to know about who she is—bold, independent, self-defining, and unfaithful—in a brief and dramatically-satisfying scene."

Keep brainstorming to find unique ways of showing. Never settle for the first idea that comes to you. Show rather than tell, and your writing will sparkle.

8| The Old Lady In The Fifth Row

One afternoon, I went to a showing of *"Casino Royale"* on Manhattan's Upper East Side. It was full of neighborhood residents in their 70s and 80s. They talked throughout the movie, commenting on events as they unfolded. After the lights went on, they sat there discussing the whole film! Fascinated, I did what any good writer does: I eavesdropped. The words I heard most often were, "I didn't get why…" and "I didn't like…" I'm sure these moviegoers see whatever is playing in the neighborhood, regardless of genre, just to get out of the house. It's a chance to meet their friends and have a social outlet. They probably knew James Bond wasn't their cup of tea when they bought their tickets, but they were still disappointed. Like all moviegoers, they had wanted to like the movie.

Becoming attuned to audience reaction is an important part of your job. As a writer, you're a people watcher, so put those people-watching skills toward your education. Go to a movie you've already seen, but this time place yourself in the very front row, off to one side. Instead of facing the screen, turn and face the audience. Notice the expressions on their faces during a tense scene. See where they get bored or where they lean over to their friends and hiss, "That would never happen!" Watching an audience watch the movie will teach you the most important lesson you can learn: your job as a screenwriter is to involve the audience every step of the way.

Do this exercise with movies you love as well as movies you hate. Do it with high-concept blockbusters, indie hits, even obscure Iranian political dramas (hey, you never know what you might learn). Do it with movies like the ones you aspire to write or in genres you work in.

Who is the audience for these films? Are they younger, older, male, or female? Are they intellectuals, average folks, or a cross-section of the population? See the same movie in different theaters, even in different cities if you get the chance. Then let this little study in human psychology inform you as you go back to your own script.

You can't please all of the people all of the time, so don't even try. But after you hear a sweet little old lady in the fifth row exclaim, "I just didn't think this James Bond was very nice," I bet you bring a different understanding of the audience to your work.

9| Watch Movies Like A Screenwriter

When most people watch a movie, they react to it on an emotional level. Did they like it? Were they transported? Did the story make them laugh or cry? They base their judgment of the movie on their subjective experience and rarely think about it beyond that.

Writer Pedro de Alcantara says, "Most moviegoers tend to take the screenplay for granted. They don't know, and don't want to know, that what they see onscreen is Dustin Hoffman speaking lines written by Avery Corman, lines further chosen and edited by Robert Benton. All they care about is Kramer fighting, Kramer making mistakes, Kramer nearly destroying his child's life. Moviegoers don't leave the theater saying to themselves, 'The subtext in the dialogue was so subtle, it gave Hoffman's character tremendous verisimilitude.' They don't use six-syllable words. They say, "That bastard! He almost screwed it up!'"

From now on when you watch a movie, notice your subjective experience as you always have. But afterwards, take a step back and look at the film more objectively.

"The writer in a permanent writerly frame of mind, goes home angry, tearful, elated—but also pondering character arc, the inciting incident in the first act, the length and variety of scenes, the point of view. Ask yourself, 'Whose story was it? Was there enough foreshadowing to prepare and justify the climax?'" says de Alcantara.

Start asking questions about what worked and what didn't. If you laughed at a joke, analyze how the punch line was set up and delivered. If you were bored, think about the movie's pacing and focus. If you didn't care enough about the main character, figure out what you would have done differently. It's always easier to spot problems in other people's work. By doing this exercise, you'll train yourself to see flaws in your own work and you'll learn to generate solutions.

10| Complex, Not Complicated

I recently read a script by a novice writer that was more like five different movies. Each of the five characters had a complicated story with enough drama to rival Jerry Springer. Keeping track of a single storyline was hard, never mind weaving them together. It was impossible to care for the characters because we didn't have time to follow any of them through a character arc. As a result, they remained two-dimensional cardboard figures.

In an effort to give their stories depth, many writers confuse complicated plot lines for complexity. They are not the same. When talking about plots and characters, complicated means confusing. Complex means intricate and interesting. Action is not story. Events are not story. We don't have story until we have a determined character with a goal who faces mounting obstacles along the way to achieving that goal.

If your hero's goal is to win the state championship, that's enough. Stay with that and find events that act as obstacles toward that goal. Don't have him also trying to solve a murder, save his girlfriend from drugs, and help his best friend launch a home-made rocket ship. Pick a single, central conflict. Choose character traits that create inner conflict. Give him a flaw that makes us worry he won't achieve his goal. Throwing in a bunch of complications is simply confusing. Do your story a favor and keep it lean.

11| Read Other Scripts

No serious writer would compose a novel without having studied and learned from dozens of novels. So why do so many beginning screenwriters neglect to study scripts of produced movies?

Reading scripts is one of the best ways to learn the craft of screenwriting. Don't skip this vital step! Download scripts of your favorite movies from the Internet. Read as many different kinds of scripts as possible, and then watch the movie while following along with the script. Notice the differences. Perhaps a scene was cut, or some dialogue was changed. See if you can figure out why. Do you think the changes improved the movie or not? If you do this exercise, you'll be able to answer many of your basic formatting questions, and you'll begin to see how screenwriters structure their stories.

Online resources for scripts

Free downloads:
http://www.script-o-rama.com
http://www.simplyscripts.com
http://www.iscriptdb.com
http://www.movie-page.com

Classics, new releases, and hard-to-find scripts at reasonable prices: http://www.scriptcity.com

Screenwriting Concepts

12| High Concept And Creativity

Coming up with a powerful high concept idea is a creative challenge that can actually improve your writing. The process forces you to hone your story. You have to get really clear on what it's about and what makes it unique and worth telling. For example, a buddy film about two homicide detectives after a gang of drug dealers might have the makings of a strong concept, but it depends on how it's executed. Right now the pitch is all "familiar" with no "unique." No one can begin to visualize a specific story. But give one of those cops a suicidal death wish and legally register him as a Lethal Weapon, like screenwriter Shane Black did, and suddenly light bulbs go off.

Producers start imagining all sorts of incredible scenes with an A-list actor in the lead. You've just elevated a strong concept to a high concept. You went from "maybe it's a movie but I can't tell for sure," to "Wow, what a movie!" And let's face it. You've just improved your story.

High concept can be gimmicky and formulaic, or it can be creatively liberating for you the writer and fresh and amazing for the audience. As a spec screenwriter, you have all the freedom in the world to ensure your script is the latter. Before you dismiss high concept as "too Hollywood," give it an honest try. You just might write your best—and most marketable—script yet.

13| First Impressions: The Title

Many screenwriters get lazy when it comes to titling their scripts. The argument is always the same: "Why bother? The studio's going to change it anyway." I can think of at least three good reasons:

Pride: The title is the first sample of your writing anyone sees. If it's boring, what does that say about you as a writer? And what's going to entice a reader to pick your script out of the pile?

Marketing: A great title makes your movie easier to market. Your title goes hand-in-hand with your logline. The logline sets up the pitch, the title delivers the clincher.

Writer's discipline: Coming up with a fantastic title means clarifying your concept. It helps you see the movie as much as it helps the producer. If you start to stray while writing or pitching, a single glance at the title can help get you back on track.

According to producer Hal Croasmun, there are three types of titles that work.

• The same title as the best-selling book that the movie is based on. This works even for titles that are confusing or uninspiring because they already have a built-in audience ("*Cold Mountain*", "*Remains of the Day*", "*The Godfather*").

• Intriguing titles that hint at something lurking underneath the surface ("*Indecent Proposal*", "*Crying Game*", "*One Flew Over The Cuckoo's Nest*").

"Avoid overly long titles, titles where you have to watch the movie to understand them, or titles that are confusing or make you think it's a different genre," advises Croasmun.

There are many ways to brainstorm great titles. Here are a couple of tips from Croasmun:

- Use contradictory word combinations, as in *"Back to the Future"* or *"Bad Santa"*.

- Give us the main character's internal state, as in *"Bedazzled"* or *"Unforgiven"*.

- Give us the key location, as in *"Moulin Rouge"*, or *"Air Force One"*.

- Use a cliché from the story, as in *"You've Got Mail"*, or a twist on a cliché in *"Natural Born Killers"*. Remember, the title is the first impression a reader gets of your writing. Make sure it shines!

14| High Concept, Characters, and Genre

High concept can leave plenty of room for originality and character. In fact, the best high-concept stories feature characters we care and cheer for. In *"Kramer vs. Kramer"*, we want to see Ted Kramer love his son and fight for him. In *"Master and Commander"*, we want Captain Jack Aubrey to win that sea battle and save the British from defeat.

Our favorite heroes are ordinary people moved to do extraordinary things (Ted Kramer), or extraordinary people with abilities beyond our own (Harry Potter). The hero's conflict usually involves both internal and external conflict. Other examples of high concepts that are strong in character are *"Almost Famous"* and *"Rain Man"*. While action films and other big-budget blockbusters are high concept, guns, car chases, and explosions aren't obligatory.

High concept is at home in every genre: romantic comedies (*"Sleepless in Seattle"*), animation (*"Chicken Run"*), thrillers (*"The Silence of the Lambs"*), indies (*"Blair Witch Project"*), classics (*"Gone with the Wind"*), and chick flicks (*"Thelma and Louise"*). Television, of course, abounds with high concepts: "Kojak", "The West Wing", "The Sopranos."

15| How To Come Up With A High Concept Idea

Anything can be an idea seed—a person you meet, an article you read, or something you experience. But once an idea seed has been planted, how can you nurture it so that it will grow into a fully-fledged concept?

The first step is to determine what fascinates you about the idea. Say you meet a construction worker. He's just an average guy, but something about him sparks your interest. If you take his typical-day-in-the-life-of-a-construction-worker tale and try to turn it into a script, chances are it won't be intriguing enough to carry a whole movie. Dig deeper to discover what really fascinates you about him. Is it the contradiction between his sheer physical strength and his gentle nature? Is it the dangerous world he inhabits, suspended hundreds of feet above the ground? Or is it the tales of municipal corruption he spins? As you can see, a single idea seed can open up multiple possibilities.

Use your fascination to brainstorm as many different story ideas as you can. Sometimes you'll decide on a concept that includes your original seed idea, but often the process takes you in a completely different direction. Allow yourself this flexibility and keep brainstorming until you come up with something truly amazing!

Learn More: If you want to master the structure for creating high concept ideas, I highly recommend Hal Croasmun's High Concept Sells class at http://scriptforsale.com.

16| The Low Down On High Concept

There are a limited number of themes that capture our collective imagination. In the end, all stories boil down to a handful of universal conflicts: life and death, good and evil, right and wrong, freedom and imprisonment, love and hate, and so on. In a sense, we're telling the same stories over and over again. But audiences quickly tire of repetition. They want fresh takes on ancient human dilemmas. That's why producers insist on stories that are "unique but familiar." They want films that grab an audience's attention within the first 10 pages and hold it until fade out.

It's in our nature to respond to original stories with compelling heroes and exciting conflicts—what we storytellers call a "strong concept." Shakespeare's plays (*Romeo and Juliet*, *Macbeth*) are based on strong concepts, as are many Greek tragedies (*Oedipus Rex*), operas (*The Marriage of Figaro*, *Aida*, *Carmen*), and countless novels (*Pride and Prejudice*, *The Firm*). The strongest concept of all is a high concept. According to producer Hal Croasmun, a high concept has three essential components:

• The concept can be told in a single sentence that helps you immediately imagine the entire movie.

• The concept is unique in a significant way.

• The concept appeals to a wide audience. The more original and appealing the idea, the higher the concept.

The crew of a deep-space mining ship is trapped on board with an extraterrestrial monster: "*Alien*". Between the title and a one-sentence pitch, we see the whole movie. Its life-and-death conflict is universal (familiar), but it's expressed in a fresh way (unique). Why is it essential that the pitch be brief? Because executives hear hundreds, if not thousands, of pitches each year. If you can paint a vivid picture with only a few words, your idea will stand out. The person you pitched it to will remember it easily and will be able to pitch it to his boss, and so on through the chain of command. If your idea is difficult to explain, it'll be hard to visualize and remember.

In some circles, high concept has developed a bad reputation as nothing but a marketing gimmick. But, as you can see by the plays and novels I mentioned above, strong concepts have been around forever. Hollywood only took the idea one step further. No matter what kind of story you strive to write—huge high-concept blockbusters like "*Pirates of the Caribbean*" or more intimate stories that are not high concept like "*Little Miss Sunshine*"—understanding what makes a strong concept is essential. If your script is original and has a great concept, it will be in demand.

17| Improving the Chances of a Not-so-Sky-High Concept

You've had a blast writing a couple of high-concept scripts that you can pitch to agents or the major studios. You now want to apply everything you've learned about storytelling to a wonderful little personal script that strays from the high concept path. If there's a market for personal spec scripts by newcomers, how can you tap into it?

A not-so-sky-high-concept script lives or dies on the quality of the writing—even more than a high-concept one. If you're ready for the challenge, however, follow entertainment lawyer Judith Merian's tips for increasing your chance of success: Keep the budget low. Cut down on or totally eliminate the following:

- The number of locations

- Stunts, explosions, and special effects

- Fancy sets, costumes, uniforms, and period pieces

- Animals

- Crowd scenes

- Too many secondary characters

Consider your niche market—and use it. Expect an initial appeal to a niche audience which means small box office numbers.

"My Big Fat Greek Wedding" was initially released in cities with Greek populations, giving the film a built-in audience and press coverage. As the word spread, so did the film's appeal. *Greek* cost $5 million and made $356 million in worldwide box office.

Write stories that travel. Write stories people can identify with, no matter where they live. A crazy family and its ugly duckling is universal. "*Little Miss Sunshine*" and "*My Big Fat Greek Wedding*" both used this theme.

Do your homework. The financiers behind "*My Big Fat Greek Wedding*" knew exactly how and to whom they could initially sell this film. Have an answer when asked, "Why should I take a chance with this offbeat story?" Be prepared to deliver data to back up your claims. Your financier is thinking ROI (return on investment) and so should you. Make it part of your pitch.

Have a marketing concept in mind. "*Little Miss Sunshine*" opened in seven theaters and expanded its release as it got good press. As it generated revenue, its distributor invested in marketing campaigns in additional cities. Its widest release was 1,602 theaters. It cost $8 million and made $84 million in worldwide theatrical release as of July 2006.

Cut down on violence, graphic sex, and raw language, all of which limit the audience even further in theaters, TV, and DVD. You want to increase the opportunities for making money, not diminish them. Addressing these elements with subtlety in the writing can enhance chances. Appeal to an actor's ego. Write a script with a particular talent in mind (or say you did), and then send a great marketing letter to his production company.

18| Test Your Concept Before You Start Writing

"I wouldn't start a screenplay without a solid concept," says screenwriter/editor Jackie Pike. "Develop your concept to carry you through three acts before you start writing." Use this checklist to test and elevate your concept:

· Is my idea universal? This isn't a matter of appealing to the lowest common denominator but of touching what is shared by all of us.

· Is your concept about something everyone has experienced, such as the death of a beloved one, the threat to life and limb, or the weight of injustice? Will the audience respond emotionally?

· Can I give my idea a unique twist? You want to write a story about a couple of bachelors who fear commitment. This is a universal theme, but we've also seen it hundreds of times. Now give the concept a twist by having the bachelor's display their party-on attitude in a unique way, and you end up with "*The Wedding Crashers*", a fresh and successful comedy written by Steve Faber and Bob Fisher.

· Is my protagonist likable? Does she elicit empathy? Will the audience care about what happens to your protagonist? In a dark piece, like "*Monster*", will your audience understand and empathize with your protagonist, even if they find her behavior despicable? Have you given her inner as well as outer conflicts? Will she have to grow in order to accomplish her goal? Are the stakes high enough?

· What will happen if your heroine doesn't achieve her goal? In "*Freaky Friday*", a mother and daughter magically switch bodies and desperately search for a way to switch back. Naturally, they each detest being in the wrong body. But screenwriters Heather Hach and Leslie Dixon raised the stakes yet another notch with a plot complication. The mother, Tess, is getting married in 24 hours. If they don't switch back in time, either the daughter, Anna, will have to go through with the wedding (unthinkable!), or Tess will lose her fiancé. Elevate the excitement of your script by elevating the stakes.

· Can I summarize my concept in a logline of 25 words or less? Distilling your idea to a 25-word logline forces you to clarify what your story is about. A clear concept keeps your screenplay on track.

· Does my title capture the spirit of my script? Give your script a title that fits with your logline and makes your script stand out from the pile. What's a reader more likely to pick up: *The Shark* or *Jaws*?

Once you've elevated your concept, pitch it to as many people as you can—your friends, your family, even strangers. If it elicits the kind of emotional response you're hoping for (laughter, chills, excitement) move on to the outlining stage. If instead you're met with polite smiles or blank stares, keep working on your concept. And don't be afraid to ditch an iffy concept altogether. The creative mind is infinitely fertile, and you'll soon come up with a new concept to test.

19| Theme

The theme of your story is its underlying issue, the thing it's about, the moral at the story's core. Theme is what transforms the film from a collection of interesting scenes to a unified whole. Theme gives the story its spine. It's the glue that binds. Think of your theme as a thesis that your protagonist will prove either right or wrong.

In "*Casablanca*" the theme is self-sacrifice for a higher purpose. Humphrey Bogart goes from insisting that he sticks his neck out for no one to sacrificing the woman he loves so that they can all battle tyranny. The theme of *"The Wizard of Oz"* is, "There's no place like home." Common themes include "Crime doesn't pay," "Power corrupts," and "Reality is illusion." How do you come up with your screenplay's theme?

Sometimes theme is present from the very start, sometimes it emerges as you write. Each writer has a source of inspiration, an aspect of life that fascinates her and that she explores through her writing. Usually, your theme springs from that well. If you've chosen a story you truly believe in, the theme will become apparent. Once you are able to articulate your theme, use that knowledge as you rewrite. Every scene, character dilemma, and event should either speak to that theme or contradict it. In many movies, the theme is stated outright early in the first act. How blatantly or how subtly you do this depends on your sensibilities and on the kind of movie you're writing. Be careful, however, not to use the theme to bash the audience over the head with a message. To loosely quote Samuel Goldwyn, movies don't deliver messages. Western Union does.

20| The First 10 Pages

Take another look at the photo of Greg Beal of the Nicholl Fellowship surrounded by over 6,000 script submissions. Now imagine you're the reader sitting in the middle of that avalanche. How much patience do you have for a story that doesn't grab you right away? I'm betting not a lot. "Readers are overworked," says producer Hal Croasmun. "Your job is to make it impossible for them to put your script down."

Hollywood's short attention span can be infuriating to writers who have poured their life's blood into their work. "Unfair!" they cry. "If a reader puts down the script after 10 pages, they'll miss the award-worthy love scene on page 53. And what about the fantastic twist at the end?" Unfortunately, by then it's too late. It's the business of readers and producers to know what will hold their audience's interest.

"I've asked over 25 producers, 'At what point in a script can you tell if it is written by a professional screenwriter?'" says Croasmun. "Many said, 'Within three pages,' and more than half said, 'On the first page.'" Don't think the public will be more generous.

Several years ago, famed editor Sol Stein conducted an informal study on book-browsing habits in mid-Manhattan bookstores. He found that most people read about three pages before either buying the book or putting it down to pick up another one. In his book "On Writing," Stein says, "Thereafter, whenever a novelist told me that his novel really got going on page 10 or 20 or 30, I had to pass on the news that his book in all likelihood was doomed."

The first 10 pages need to introduce us to the story, the setting, and the characters. They need to establish the hero's "life as usual" and to show us the event that catapults the hero into a different life (inciting incident). By the end of the first 10 pages, we need to know what the story is about. All this needs to happen in a fresh and entertaining way.

Many novice writers stop the story to establish the characters and the setting and to unroll "life as usual." But experienced writers reveal character and establish relationships and setting and get the story rolling by giving us conflict from the get-go, saturating every line of dialogue with meaning, having their characters interact with the setting, and creating intriguing story questions that pique curiosity.

The best way to learn how to write great openings is by studying the first few pages of some of your favorite scripts. When you grab your reader on the first page, you've just made a promise to tell him a great story. Live up to that promise on every page that follows, and your reader won't be able to put your script down.

21| Anticipation

When my brother and I were little, my father used to tell us bedtime stories featuring Doctor Terrible, a villain of his own invention, and me and my brother as the heroes. Each night, my father would get us into an impossible predicament. There we were, trapped by Doctor Terrible and armed only with tennis rackets. We listened to my father's words, breathless with anticipation, eager to learn what ingenious plan we would hit upon. And then it would happen. My dad would turn the light off and say, "To be continued tomorrow." Mine was a sleep-deprived childhood, hanging out there on that cliff. All I could think about was WHAT WILL HAPPEN NEXT.

When you anticipate something, you look forward to it, like a special night out or a vacation, or you prepare for it, like a job interview or retirement. Anticipation propels you into the future, and the emotions about the upcoming event can range from hope and excitement to dread and worry. In real life, most of us find swinging back and forth between the two extremes too stressful. But at the movies, we find it exciting. We want to be kept on the edge of our seats hoping the hero will make it but worrying he won't.

A gripping story uses anticipation to keep us hooked. There are many ways to build anticipation into your story. One scene I saw recently did both of these to great effect. In the movie "*Babel*" (written by Guillermo Arriaga) we know that Cate Blanchett's character will be shot. We see the kids aim at the bus and pull the trigger. Then we go back in time a little and see Cate Blanchett and Brad Pitt on the bus. She's sleeping, her head against the window. We KNOW the bullet will penetrate the window, and we wait for it to happen. But she continues to sleep peacefully, oblivious to the danger, as the bus rolls on. And rolls on. The moment of impact is delayed and you're left squirming in your seat with anticipation.

After you've written a scene, go back through it and see how you can create more anticipation. Where can you make us hope the character will achieve his goal, and where can you make us worry that he won't? How many different ways can you make us ask what will happen, if it will happen, and when will it happen? Build anticipation into your script and your reader won't be able to put it down.

22| Inciting Incident, Crisis, Climax, and Resolution

The Inciting Incident is that event which disturbs the hero's life-as-he-knew-it and "incites" him to take action. It happens early in Act I, usually somewhere in the first 10 pages. In *Kramer vs. Kramer* (novel by Avery Corman, script by Robert Benton) it's when Joanna walks out and leaves Ted to parent his son alone. The Crisis is that moment when all seems lost. Nothing the hero has been doing has worked, and he's further from his goal than ever. This is the point where the hero has to regroup and rethink. Only if he digs deep and taps his inner resources will he find a strategy that works.

In *Kramer vs. Kramer*, when Ted learns he lost custody, he must choose between appealing, which would mean putting his son on the stand, or accepting the decision, which would protect Billy. He chooses to give up custody and protect Billy, and now must come to terms with the consequences. The Climax is the final showdown between the protagonist and the antagonist. This is the scene the audience has been waiting for, the moment that answers the story's biggest question. Will good triumph over evil? Will the boy get the girl? In *Kramer vs. Kramer*, the climax happens when Joanna realizes that Ted is a better father than she is a mother because he's willing to act in Billy's best interest, and she lets him have the boy. The Resolution is where all the loose ends are tied up. Often, we are left with a slight hint of the future. In *Kramer vs. Kramer*, the resolution is simple and quick: Joanna asks to be allowed to visit Billy, and then she and Ted go upstairs to talk to him. The audience is left believing that somehow, this family will find a balance that works for them.

23| Turning Points

Turning points are events that spin (or turn) the story in a new direction. They are the major twists or surprises that keep audiences glued to their seats. It takes a minimum of three turning points—one at the end of each act—to keep the audience involved through a three-act, feature-length film. Turning points are also called plot points, major reversals, or act climaxes.

At the Act I turning point, the protagonist has experienced a major change in his life and has made an initial decision about how he will respond.

At the Act II turning point, the protagonist realizes his strategy isn't working and he needs to change course.

The Act III turning point is the movie's climax, the final show-down between protagonist and antagonist. It's here that we discover whether the hero wins or loses. Many writers add a mid-act climax halfway through Act II, called the midpoint. Essentially, this is a fourth turning point, but smaller in scope than the turning point at the end of Act II. It gives the screenwriter one more destination to work toward, ensures that the conflict will build continuously, and helps keep the screenplay on track.

We expect good stories to have turning points and are disappointed when they don't. If you want to keep your audience involved, it's crucial to understand turning points.

24| Beats, Scenes, And Scene Sequences

A beat is the smallest structural unit of a script and is defined as an exchange of action/reaction. It's a line of dialogue, an action, or a reaction that creates an emotional moment. For example, a woman dressed for an evening out checks the clock—her date is late.

She's annoyed (beat #1). The doorbell rings. Angry, she opens the door (beat #2). Her date tumbles in, bloodied and bruised. Her anger turns to horror and concern (beat #3). As we see from this example, beats are strung together to build a scene.

A scene is a continuous action in a single location. Each scene functions as a mini-story, with a beginning, middle, and end. A scene has its own protagonists. This could be the hero, the antagonist, or some other character depending on the scene's purpose. The scene's protagonist must have a goal (she wants to go out) and face obstacles (her date is first late, then incapacitated). Scenes accomplish the following tasks:

- Create anticipation and move the story forward

- Reveal conflict

- Reveal character

- Elicit emotion

The best scenes accomplish several tasks at a time. Once you've clarified a scene's dramatic purpose, set it visually and dynamically. Keep your script tight by narrowing the timeframe of its action: Start the scene as late within the action being depicted as possible, and end it as soon as possible, leaving the moviegoer to imagine part of the scene's buildup and aftermath.

Scenes link together to form sequences. A scene sequence is made up of several scenes that work together to build tension toward a bigger climax. In a sequence in which the hero's wife leaves him, scene one could be an argument during which he pushes her. In scene two, he calls from work to apologize but she says she's leaving. In scene three, he rushes home to find her gone. Each scene has a climax—the push, the wife's announcement, the realization she's gone. But they all contributed toward the climax of the sequence—his realization that she's gone.

An act is constructed out of scenes and scene sequences that build toward a climax bigger than each of the scene sequence climaxes. The information revealed in an act climax is so new and shocking that it completely changes the protagonist's situation.

25| Exposition

Sometimes viewers need to know about something that happened before the movie began so they can understand the story. Or they need some background information on a character that explains his personality or behavior. Exposition, as this information is called, has to be delivered through setups, flashbacks, dialogue, or other subtle means, including visuals and music.

Writing exposition is tricky, because it can easily fall in the "telling" rather than "showing" mode. If you're too heavy-handed with your exposition, you pull the reader out of the fictional world. Good exposition is woven naturally into the story. Exposition should be doled out on a "need to know" basis. Give the reader only as much as he needs to know right now in order to understand the story.

A good way of creating suspense and masking exposition at the same time is by making the audience curious about what happened or what the character is hiding. In "*Casablanca*," by the time the flashback of Rick and Ilsa in Paris rolls around, we are dying to know what happened between them. One trick for revealing information the audience needs to know is to reveal it to a character who is also in the dark. In "*The Silence of the Lambs*" (novel by Thomas Harris, script by Ted Tally), Clarice's superior prepares her to meet Lecter. Because Clarice needs this information to do her job and stay safe, this bit of exposition comes across as believable.

A more awkward bit of exposition is the opening scene of "*My Best Friend's Wedding.*" At dinner with George, Julianne checks her answering machine and learns her best friend Michael called. She then proceeds to tell George every detail we need to know about her relationship with Michael. The problem is, George is Julianne's second-best friend. Wouldn't he already know the story? That kind of information dump is pure telling. It pulls you out of the story.

Another trick is to reveal exposition through action. In "*Casino Royale*" (novel by Ian Fleming, screenplay by Neal Purvis, Robert Wade, and Paul Haggis) a scene was included to inform us of Bond's double-00 status, achieved once a spy kills twice. Bond is face-to-face with a spy gone bad. The spy is cautious but confident, sure that if he were really in trouble, the agency would have sent a double-00 agent. But, as he points out, Bond has only killed once. At that point, Bond pulls out a gun and shoots him, securing his double-00 status.

When writing exposition, search for ways to mask it. Don't tell us anything we don't need to know, and don't allow characters to discuss things they already know. Reveal exposition through action as much as you can. And create curiosity by holding on to exposition until it's absolutely essential to the story.

26| Writing Narrative

Narrative is everything that isn't dialogue. It includes descriptions of the characters, the locations, the images and actions we see, and the sounds we hear. It also sets mood, pace, and tone. Good narrative is active and lean. Here are some points to keep in mind:

· **Write only what you can see or hear**. If you describe a character's inner state (A painful memory from when he was 5 years old overwhelms George) or give backstory (Celia was Jonathan's first girlfriend) in the narrative, how will the audience be made aware of this information? If it's absolutely vital to the story to have this information, turn it into a visual or a line of dialogue.

· **Describing Actions**. Whereas novels are often written in past tense, screenplays are always written as if they're happening right here, right now.

· **Use present tense**: John opens the door, walks into the room. **Stick to active voice**: John opens the door, and **avoid the passive voice**: The door was opened by John. Replace the present continuous (Gloria is driving) with the present simple (Gloria drives) whenever you can.

- **Describing Characters**. When describing the way a character looks, avoid non-descriptive clichés like "drop-dead gorgeous," or specifics like "blond and blue-eyed." The first only gives us a generic picture, and the second limits the casting possibilities. Use metaphors to paint more vivid pictures. Instead of, "At six feet tall and weighing only 120 pounds, Beth is too skinny," say "If Beth stood sideways and stuck out her tongue, she'd look like a zipper."

- **Break up the paragraphs**. Large blocks of text are a turn-off to the reader. First, it slows down the reading experience and as a result slows down the story. Second, it indicates the writer is either inexperienced or spending too much time on details.

- Keep your description to blocks of four or five lines. Include only details that are truly important. Keep your sentences short and simple. Avoid complicated grammatical constructions.

- **Tone**: Keep your tone consistent. If you're writing a comedy, your descriptions, actions, and choice of words should be funny, too. If you're writing an action film, then your narrative should be full of tension and action.

27| Story Is Conflict

There is no story without conflict. As entertainment lawyer Judith Merians puts it, "Too often writers forget to tell a story. There's lots of character development, establishing of setting, but I don't know what the fight's about. If I don't know that, you've lost me."

When a character wants something very badly but must overcome obstacles to get it, this creates an interplay of opposing forces—in other words, conflict. Conflict is about struggling for power in ways big or small. Luke Skywalker wants to beat Darth Vader. Three bachelors taking care of a baby want it to stop crying. The stakes may be different, but both are power struggles that give a story its essential conflict. The choices a person makes when faced with extreme conflict bring out his or her deepest character. That's why conflict is so compelling dramatically. We get to live through the hero's dilemma vicariously and wonder if we ourselves would be as courageous or as foolish. There are four elements essential for story conflict:

• The character must have a goal and encounter obstacles along the way.

• The goal must be essential to the character. He must not be willing to give up. There can be no compromise.

• The goal can't be too easy to achieve. The odds should be stacked against him.

• The character must stand SOME hope of achieving it, otherwise the story will come across as implausible.

Every story has a central conflict. In *"The Pursuit of Happyness*, written by Steve Conrad, the central conflict is Chris Gardner's struggle to become a stockbroker and provide a home for his 5-year-old son. But there's also scene conflict: between Chris and the mother of his son, who doesn't believe in him; when Chris is in the homeless shelter repairing his last bone density scanner so he can sell it to feed his son, and the shelter lights go out; and when Chris' boss asks to borrow $5 without realizing it's all Chris has left. Each of these scene conflicts feed the primary conflict. Chris can't give up or his son will go hungry. The odds are highly stacked against him and his goal seems almost impossible to achieve. But he has two qualities that give us hope: He's determined, and he's highly intelligent.

Start with the primary conflict, which is your hero's story goal. As your story progresses, add new obstacles and setbacks for your character to overcome, but make sure each conflict feeds the bigger conflict. Allow the obstacles to become increasingly more difficult and the conflict to escalate as the hero approaches the crisis point. Master the art of conflict, and you will have the audience sitting on the edge of their seats.

28| External And Internal Conflict

As contests go, a boxing match is pretty straightforward: two guys (usually) beat each other until one falls down and can't get up. This is primeval conflict—man against man in violent confrontation. Because violence is so unambiguous, movies featuring this kind of conflict resonate with everyone and therefore do well globally. But violence isn't the only kind of conflict there is—or even the most common.

Movie heroes battle individuals, groups, natural and supernatural forces, or their own inner demons. When a protagonist is forced to face his own flaws, this is known as "internal conflict." All other conflict can be grouped together as "external conflict." Because movies are a visual medium, the most successful screen stories depict external conflict represented by a visible, tangible external antagonist.

Films with external conflicts include "*When Harry Met Sally*" (man against man), "*Jaws*" (man against nature), "*Rosemary's Baby*" (man against the supernatural), and "*Erin Brockovich*" (man against society). But movies are rendered more interesting when they include internal conflict in addition to the external one.

The most gripping stories include external situations or antagonists that force a hero to face and conquer his character flaws in order to succeed. In "*The Verdict*", written by Barry Reed and David Mamet, Paul Newman plays an alcoholic lawyer who must overcome his inner demons and win a groundbreaking case against a corrupt institution. The internal conflict deepens the external conflict and strengthens the movie.

Boxing matches are only compelling because we get caught up in the drama of watching an underdog dig deep within himself to muster the strength to win. We are awed by the sheer determination exhibited by the combatants, and wonder if we have that same ability inside ourselves. Effective internal conflict can range from overcoming awkwardness or insecurity ("*The 40 Year Old Virgin*") to struggling with addiction ("*Leaving Las Vegas*") or madness ("*Shine*"), but in order to be dramatic, it must be expressed visually.

29| Conflict And Status Negotiation

Certain schools of acting teach that every human interaction boils down to a negotiation for status. Every gesture made, word spoken, and action taken is an attempt to either elevate or lower one's status in relation to the other person. If you think about it for a moment, you'll see just how true that is.

In a shop one day I watched a woman walk up to a cashier and ask for a pack of cigarettes. The shop was out of her brand. Most people would pick a different one or go to another store, but not this lady. She insisted. The cashier glanced at the line forming and, somewhat vexed, repeated they were out. The woman tried to engage the cashier in conversation. She didn't seem to mind holding everyone up. She felt she deserved attention, and she wasn't going to allow the cashier to lower her status by depriving her of it. But from the cashier's point of view, her own status was being lowered. She prided herself on her efficiency, and this customer was keeping her from doing her job. She snapped at the customer—which only led the customer to greater hesitancy and indecision. Meanwhile, everyone in line was grumbling. I'm sure they felt the customer was wasting their time—and lowering their status. Finally, the manager came over. He led the woman away to another register, where he indulged her. From his point of view, as manager and mediator, his higher status remained intact. From the customer's point of view, her status as someone worthy of attention and service also remained intact. They both felt they had the upper hand. When I left, the customer was still happily browsing cigarettes.

And me? As the detached writer/observer, I found my own way of maintaining status by choosing to thrive on the situation rather than becoming exasperated by it.

Some status negotiations seem obvious: a prisoner and a warden, a teacher and a student, a king and a peasant. But status negotiations occur in every relationship, no matter how loving or intimate. Mothers and daughters, brothers and sisters, husbands and wives continually jockey for the upper hand. We even manage to elevate our status by seemingly lowering it. Witness a group of women complaining about their ailments. "You think you've got it bad? I can hardly walk!" The one with the worst ailment seems to be lowering her status, but in fact she's proclaiming herself champion in the battle of pain.

Create conflict by infusing every character interaction, no matter how mundane, with status negotiation. Don't forget status negotiations between grown-ups and children, and between pets and their owners. ***Learn more***: Read Impro, by famed acting teacher Keith Johnstone.

30| Genre

Stories are arranged by their shared elements into categories called genres. Aristotle gave us the first two genres by organizing stories according to their emotional charge. Positive or upbeat stories were categorized as "fortunate." Negative or downbeat ones were "tragic." As storytelling evolved over the centuries, more and more genres and subgenres emerged. Today, no one can agree on how many genres exist or how to divide them. Below is a description of some of the most common film genres and subgenres. All of these will be familiar to you and, as you will see, genres often overlap.

Comedy: This category includes romantic (*There's Something About Mary*) and screwball comedies (*Rat Race*), satires (*Thank You for Smoking*), and black comedies (*Catch-22*). Comedies are meant to amuse. Since it's hard to laugh at someone in danger, one of the most important rules of comedy is that no one gets hurt. No matter how many pratfalls a character takes, his reaction is always funnier than the injury is painful. The only exception is black comedy, where the scale tips toward laughs of discomfort.

Drama: Drama is an umbrella category for a serious portrayal of realistic characters, settings, and situations—in other words, everything that isn't a comedy. The important distinction here is the emotional charge. Comedies make us smile, laugh, and guffaw; dramas make us reflect, worry, and cry. The category drama has many subsets and includes movies like *Kramer vs. Kramer*, *The English Patient*, and *Rain Man*.

Action/Adventure: Action films are fast-paced, mile-a-minute rides. Explosions, chases, and battles figure prominently. Adventure films usually revolve around some kind of quest, and are often set in exotic locales. Action and adventure are so intertwined that they are often treated as one. Some sub-genres are: disaster/survival films (*The Day After Tomorrow*), treasure hunts (*Romancing the Stone*), swashbucklers (*Pirates of the Caribbean*), and spy films (*Casino Royale*).

Crime: Here, the main storyline revolves around a crime committed. Among this category's many sub-genres are: police dramas (*Se7en*), gangster films (*The Untouchables*), film noir (*The Maltese Falcon*), courtroom dramas (*12 Angry Men*), and thrillers (*The Manchurian Candidate*).

Horror: Designed to scare the living daylights out of us, horror films shock and thrill at the same time. In his book "Story: Substance, Structure, Style and The Principles of Screenwriting," Robert McKee divides horror into three subgenres: the uncanny, in which the source of horror is subject to rational explanation (*Psycho*), the supernatural, in which the source of horror is irrational or from the spirit world (*Poltergeist*), or the super-uncanny, where the audience is kept guessing between the two other possibilities.

Learn more: The genres above are only one way of classifying story types. For a thought-provoking take on the issue, check out Blake Snyder's book Save the Cat.

31| Genre Conventions

"Understand the conventions of the genre you're writing for," says screenwriter Susannah Farrow. "There are certain things moviegoers expect to see in a comedy and other things they expect to see in a thriller. Make sure you include those things." Audiences have their favorite genres and are well versed in genre conventions. If they've come to see a comedy, they want laughs. But they also want original situations, not something they've seen a hundred times. To write successfully within a genre, a writer must study and master its conventions while avoiding its cliché. The choice of genre may impose conventions on:

• setting (the West in a western, a battle in a war film)

• roles (detective and criminal in a detective story)

• events (boy-meets-girl in a love story)

• emotional expectations (in an action/adventure, will the hero save the day? In a horror movie, will the axe murderer strike again?).

Some genres have many conventions. Let's take a crime story as an example. The audience expects: a crime to occur early on; someone to investigate; twists in the form of false clues, multiple suspects, or the revelation of hidden layers; and a showdown (physical, intellectual, or both) between the criminal and the investigator. The hardest part of writing within a genre is avoiding its cliché. The first writer who revealed that the criminal was really a corrupt cop found an exciting, new twist. But by now that device has become an overused gimmick.

Find ways of meeting audience expectations without resorting to cliché. Watch as many movies in your genre as you can, and study their scripts. Ask the following questions:

• What are the conventions of settings, roles, and events?

• What emotional expectations are the films fulfilling?

• What's been done to death?

• What's original?

• How is your script like these movies, and how does it differ?

• Can you give the events that have to happen in your story a fresh, contemporary twist without committing any genre sins or falling into formulaic writing?

Understanding genre is an essential element of good writing. If you master your genre and its conventions, you'll be able to pay off audience expectation with skill, originality, and elegance. And if you wish to write a genre-defying script, your knowledge of genre will only make your experiment bolder.

32| Setups And Payoffs

Think of setup as a promise made and payofs as a promise fulfilled. When you set something up, you create an expectation in the reader that it'll be paid off later. In *Thelma and Louise*, as Thelma is packing, she throws in her gun on a whim, even though she has never used it and is afraid of it. When we see that, it propels us into the future. We know that gun is going to be used and wait for it to happen. If it doesn't, we'll feel cheated.

Every story element needs to be set up: actions, character traits, character transformations, events, turning points, the ending. In *The Pursuit of Happyness*, set in the 1980s, we see the hero playing with a Rubik's cube, and we hear a report on TV about the fad its set off (setup). In a later scene, the hero attempts to talk himself into a prestigious training program for stockbrokers, but the broker he's trying to impress is too wrapped up in the Rubik's cube to listen. The hero manages to complete the puzzle, thereby proving his smarts to the stockbroker (payoff). When you set something up, it needs to evolve organically and naturally.

The point is to tease without blatantly manipulating. It can't scream, "Hey, you! Look here!" Make the intervening stuff between the setup and the payoff pertinent to the story and interesting in its own right. Then deliver the payoff. Work on getting the timing right, which will vary from scene to scene and story to story. Don't leave people hanging too long, but don't close the gap too quickly either.

33| Subplots

Subplots are secondary storylines that either support or contrast the theme of the main storyline. If your theme is a thesis that your protagonist will prove either right or wrong, then the subplots are the different sides of the argument. They're the pros and cons.

Supporting the thesis through one storyline and contradicting it through another enriches the story and generates curiosity about how the protagonist will resolve his dilemma. What will he choose? How will it turn out? Subplots also help give us a better sense of character.

One of the subplots in the movie *Moonstruck* (written by John Patrick Shanley) involves the main character's parents. Loretta's mother discovers that her husband, whom she truly loves, is having an affair. This subplot mirrors and plays out the theme, which is true love is a risk worth taking. Her mother's story underscores Loretta's dilemma: Will she play it safe in a loveless marriage? Or will she follow her heart and embrace vulnerability, as her mother did?

Subplots are complete stories with a beginning, middle, and end. They have their own protagonists, usually a secondary character. The subplot protagonist often goes through a change, but it's a shift rather than a profound transformation. That kind of journey is reserved for the hero. Your decisions about where and how to begin and end your subplots will affect the pace of your entire story. You may want to have the major subplot climax coincide with the A-story climax, or slightly before or after. Be careful not to dilute the A-story climax. Be sure to wrap up any loose subplot threads in the resolution.

34| Organize Your Story In Three Acts

Storytellers have employed the three-act structure since its origins in ancient Greek drama, and Hollywood still uses it today as its standard. While it isn't the only way to successfully organize a story, it's a good place to start, particularly since studio executives pretty much expect it. And, once you have mastered the three-act structure, you'll be able to play with alternative structures much more convincingly.

The three-act structure is an organizational tool. Every good story has dramatic tension that happens at the right time and in the right places. Too little tension, and the story stalls. Too much tension, and you wind up overwhelming and confusing your audience. The three-act structure helps you map out the progression of tension from opening to inciting incident to climax and resolution in a coherent way.

Each of the acts has a specific job to do. You can think of it as setup, complications, and resolution. Or to put it another way, get your hero up a tree in the first act, throw progressively bigger rocks at him and force him further up the tree in the second, and let him climb down or shake him out of the tree in the third. Let's take a closer look at the individual acts.

35| Setting the Tension: Act I

Act I sets the tension and gets the hero up the tree by establishing the characters, the story world, the story concept, and the conflict. We learn who the protagonist is and what he wants. We become familiar with his world before it gets disrupted, and we are encouraged to like him or feel sympathy toward him. We also learn where and when the story is taking place and are introduced to the rules of this story world. An event must happen in Act I to disrupt our protagonist's life, eliciting action from him and setting the story in motion. This is the inciting incident, and it often occurs early in the first act. The first major twist or reversal in the story occurs at the end of Act I. The protagonist has experienced a major change in his life and has made an initial decision about how to react to this change. The conflict has been established.

The first act of *Thelma and Louise* (written by Callie Khouri) introduces us to the two protagonists and their normal world. Their goal at this point is a weekend away, a bit of an escape from the daily grind. For Louise (Susan Sarandon), it's a break from waitressing and an opportunity to get her mind off Jimmy, her non-committal boyfriend. For Thelma (Geena Davis), it's a chance to escape her domineering husband. When they stop at a bar for a few drinks, we experience their bond and their sense of humor, and we quickly get to like them. The inciting incident occurs when Louise shoots the man attempting to rape a drunken Thelma in the bar's parking lot, disrupting life as they knew it in a dramatic way. By then we're on their side, ready to follow their adventure. Generally speaking, Act I covers the first 25-30 pages of the screenplay.

36| Building the Tension: Act II

Act II throws rocks at the hero by building the tension and deepening the conflict until the tension reaches a breaking point at the end of the act. The protagonist now has a goal—to get the girl, solve the mystery, save the world. If he achieves his goal without struggle, we have no story. So the writer throws obstacles in the hero's way and develops subplots to complicate his life.

By the end of Act II, the hero has his goal in sight and thinks he has the solution. But then the major reversal at the end of Act II turns his solution on its head. The hero is forced to muster even more strength and determination or change his plan, often against a running clock. In the second act of *Thelma and Louise*, the girls now have a different goal: to escape to Mexico.

Their main obstacle becomes the law. Complications build. They need money. Louise refuses to go through Texas. The law is closing in on them. But finally Louise's boyfriend Jimmy shows up with some cash and it looks like they'll make it—until a hitchhiker Thelma picked up robs them at the Act II turning point. Act II generally runs from page 25 or 30 to about page 90.

37| Accelerating And Then Releasing The Tension: Act III

Act III gets the hero out of the tree by accelerating the action. Now we're on a downhill ride as the hero makes a new plan and goes for broke. All the complications the screenwriter established during Acts I and II come together in Act III. At the climax, the hero will either land safely or he'll crash and burn. In the aftermath following the climax, the tension releases. Any threads that are still left hanging are resolved, and we catch a glimpse of the hero's future. We finally find out if he gets the girl, or if he lands in jail.

The third act of *Thelma and Louise* accelerates the action: Thelma robs a store; the girls blow up a semi; they refuse to turn themselves in even though the law is closing in on them. At the climax, a chase scene involving multiple cop cars ensues—and leaves the girls hanging on the edge of a cliff. In this film, climax and resolution happen almost simultaneously when the girls decide to go over the cliff rather than turn themselves in. Act III covers the last 25 or 30 pages of the screenplay. The overall movement in a three-act screenplay can be stated as first setting tension, then building it, and finally accelerating and releasing it.

The lengths of the acts as stated above (a ratio of 1:2:1) are flexible. In fact, it is often dramatically advisable to shorten Act III. Ideally, Act III should give the audience a sense of acceleration up to the final conflict and finish with a resolution that is short and sweet. An Act III that is too long will drag the story down.

38| The End: Inevitable And Surprising

The ending is the last thing an audience sees. If it's amazing, they'll remember the movie as a wonderful experience. If not, they'll leave the theater disappointed.

There are three kinds of endings. Happy endings, downer endings, and bittersweet endings.

Happy ending: Boy gets girl (*You've Got Mail*), justice triumphs (*The Verdict*), and everyone lives happily ever after. We leave the theater feeling good, our hearts full of hope for humanity and ourselves. Because audiences love happy endings, Hollywood loves happy endings.

Downer endings: Boy gets girl but he loses something even more valuable (*Body Heat*), evil has destroyed good (*Chinatown*). The world is a mess, and we leave the theater sobered. Sometimes hardship elucidates life, and there have always been successful movies with downer endings.

Bittersweet endings: Girl loses boy, but she wins something more valuable (*My Best Friend's Wedding*). Or good triumphs over evil, but only because the hero made a personal sacrifice (*Casablanca*).

Endings must resolve the story question in a clear and unambiguous way. If the question raised in Act I was, "Will the boy get the girl?" your Act III has to answer with a yes or a no. Not a maybe. Even in a bittersweet ending, the answer is either "yes, but" or "no, but."

The ending has to be set up step-by-step. It can't come out of left field. It should be hinted at throughout the film. It should feel inevitable, as if that's the only possible way this story could have ended. It should make sense. But at the same time, the ending needs to be surprising.

What? How can an ending be both inevitable and surprising?

Look at *Thelma and Louise* again. Everything in the story points to Thelma and Louise not being willing to give up their freedom. Their whole journey has been about escaping from society's constraints. Are they really going to allow themselves to go to jail? No! They have to get away! That's the inevitable part. But the *way* they choose to get away—by going over the cliff and facing their death on their own terms—*that's* the surprise.

Once you've written your ending, go back through Acts I and II and verify that every twist, event, and revelation in Act III is properly set up. This is what will make your ending seem inevitable, and therefore true to the story. It will feel right.

39| Stage Directions

Stage directions tell an actor *how* to execute the actions of the story. An example:

Sally nods. (Action.) She wants him to know she understands. (Stage direction.)

The consensus in Hollywood is that too many stage directions slow down the script reading and insult the actors' intelligence. The same goes for including camera angles in your script, a big no-no and a sign of a rank amateur. Camera angles amount to stage directions for the director. Remember, nobody likes being told how to do their job.

Writers often feel that stage directions get the emotions across expediently. If someone is speed-reading, the parenthetical will tell them Carol is feeling hurt. The reader will get it. Isn't that the point?

Yes. And no. The reader needs to be gently guided by the story itself, not pounded over the head by the writer. Similarly, the actor's motivation, the director's cues, and the designer's inspiration should all come *from within the story*. Film people are creative people. They want to fill out the details with their own imagination and creativity. A screenwriter's job is to remain evocative rather than absolute.

Let's look at an example from *Tender Mercies,* written by Horton Foote.

Mac, an alcoholic musician, wakes up alone in a motel room. Prior to abandoning him in a drunken heap, his companion went through Mac's jacket and stole his money. In this scene, Mac looks for his money to pay Rosa Lee, the owner of the motel:

He enters. He goes to a jacket lying on the floor. He searches the pockets of the jacket looking for money, but finds nothing. There is a half-empty bottle of whiskey on the dresser, and he goes to it and takes a swig and then goes back outside.

We are told what Mac does, but not how he does it. Mac doesn't stumble as he enters or search his pockets in a panic. We understand Mac intended to pay. His drinking from the bottle shows a need to steady himself, and we can assume he feels pretty bad. The actor (Robert Duvall) found his own facial expressions, timing, and gestures to communicate his character's emotions.

Focus on showing through events and actions rather than telling through stage directions. Then, if you feel a stage direction is necessary to emphasize or clarify a moment, go ahead and use it. If you do this judiciously, nobody will have a problem with it. But avoid camera angles at all costs. Simply show us what we need to see. Instead of *CLOSE UP on a hand turning a key,* write *A hand turning a key*.

Scaling back stage directions shows that you trust your story to do its job, and that you trust readers, actors, and directors to do theirs. The most confident writers use the fewest stage directions.

40| A Character's Voice

The year is 1941 in Morocco. Ilse (Ingrid Bergman) is caught in a bind between her love for Rick (Humphrey Bogart) and duty to her Resistance leader husband, Victor (Paul Henreid), whom she admires and respects. How does the ultra-cool Rick express his affection for her?

He says: "Here's looking at you, kid."

Compare this to Victor's line: "I love you very much, my dear."

Even if you've never seen Casablanca, you get a good picture of the differences between the two men.

Each character should have a distinct voice. By "voice" I don't mean only a character's accent or dialect, or whether the sound of his voice is thin, squeaky, or gruff. I also mean his personality—his character traits, and his outlook on life. Through his reactions, word choice, and speech pattern, a character's dialogue reveals where he is from, his level of education, his character, and his point of view.

Voice can be used to connect a character to others or to keep him apart. A common language will play a bigger role the closer your characters are, but for dramatic purposes, your major characters must remain distinct. Three soldiers might share certain speech patterns and use the same military jargon, for example. This connects them, identifies them as part of the same group. But they are still individuals. Maybe one is an optimistic Texan, the other a cynical New Yorker, and the third a cowardly Midwesterner. Even if characters come from the same state, same town, or the same family, their personalities will be different. They will respond differently to the same situation, choose different words, and have different speech patterns. Let's say you have a pair of lovers you want to connect.

If you rely on similar personalities or voices to accomplish this, you risk creating a superficial and boring connection rather than a compelling one of dramatic substance. Differentiate their personalities—and hence, their voices—and connect them instead through conflict. Pit one against the other or create some friction between them, and you'll have a much more dynamic scene. Take a few pages from your screenplay and delete all speaker attributions. Then show it to a friend and ask her to determine which characters are saying each line. If she can't tell one character from the other, then you need to re-think your dialogue.

41| Character Arc

At the beginning of the story, Little Red Riding Hood is a sweet, innocent thing. But we know that by the third act she'll be tough or she'll be toast. Her evolution is called a character arc. It's one of the most important elements of storytelling, and for a simple reason: when a character grows, we experience her change vicariously and are transformed along with her. We get involved with a character because we want to know if his dilemma will change him. Will it force him to overcome a deep flaw ("*Liar, Liar*"), realize his potential ("*Rocky*"), or heal an emotional wound ("*Silence of the Lambs*")?

We want to see the hero grow and change, because it gives us hope for ourselves. The character needs to be capable of change from the very beginning, otherwise the change won't ring true.

Take "*Rocky*," written by Sylvester Stallone. Rocky Balboa is an underdog. The odds are stacked against him, but he's determined. It's this quality that will help him transform from a nobody to someone who has achieved his potential. The change has to happen gradually. If it's too sudden, it will seem forced and implausible.

Another way to think of the character arc is as a map of your character's beginning, middle, and end. Your character might start off as selfish, like Jack Nicholson in *"As Good as it Gets"* (written by Mark Andrus and James L. Brooks).

As the story progresses, he faces situations and conflicts that increase his self-awareness. By the end of the movie, the character has let go of his original identity and has become more generous and thoughtful.

Make sure that at least your protagonist has an arc. Depending on your story, the antagonist and some of the supporting characters might have arcs too. A character arc doesn't necessarily require improvement. If you're going for a down ending, your protagonist will change for the worse (*"Chinatown," "Raging Bull"*).

42| Character Traits

When developing characters, many writers draw up detailed character profiles. But a list of individual events or details about a person doesn't necessarily lead to understanding.

Consider your own relationships when thinking about characters. I once dated a man for three years. Although I knew many things about him, I never fully understood him. In contrast, there have been other people in my life I understood perfectly without needing to know their every detail.

When creating characters, search for their dominant traits, not the details. "Think of people you know down to the core," says writer and producer Hal Croasmun. "You can predict how they'll react to situations and you can tell when they are out of character. The core isn't a whole compilation of details. It is the part of each person that is always present."

Think of the people in your life as characters. Let's use my ex-boyfriend as an example. One of his dominant traits was to be elusive. No matter what happened, I could never predict his reaction—other than knowing it would surprise me. One of my brother's dominant traits is he's trusting. He approaches every situation with an attitude of openness and a smile. Another of his dominant traits is self-confidence. Do you see how, together, "trusting" and "confident" already begin to paint a fuller character picture?

A trusting man who isn't confident could easily be taken advantage of. But a man who's trusting because he's secure in himself is a different story.

One of my brother's details happens to be that he's a fourth-degree black belt in karate. But that detail alone doesn't make him confident. A person might acquire a high level of proficiency in karate in order to hide his insecurities without ever achieving true confidence.

Details contribute to character traits or are shaded by them, but they don't define character. If it helps you, write extensive character profiles. But keep in mind that, in the end, we know people through a few dominant traits that are revealed in everything they say and do.

43| Create Roles Actors Love

Actors love well-written characters as much as audiences do. The A-list actor sees an Oscar nomination in your accomplished drama. The budding starlet looks at your moving coming-of-age piece and sees her big break. And someone who has been typecast sees his chance to shift directions with your knee-slapping comedy.

"When actors read a script, what they're looking for is a particular moment where they really get to chew on something interesting," says director Randa Haines. "They're looking for that moment people will remember. They want a role that stimulates them and expands their range. That's true for all parts, even supporting roles and cameos."

If you want to attract actors, make every character in your script special or engaging in some way. Give each character an agenda that is related to the main storyline and doesn't detract from it. Make sure each character is memorable in some way. Maybe they use colorful language or have a quirk or a trait that stands out.

A good example is Danny DeVito's character in *"Romancing the Stone"* (written by Diane Thomas). He's the bad guy's flunky, but he has a goal of his own, namely to quit while he's ahead. And he's very funny. He's a fully developed character in his own right, but his storyline is there to serve the main storyline.

A word of warning: roles that actors love aren't written specifically for them as actors, but for the archetypes they like playing: the reluctant hero (Tom Hanks), the shady shapeshifter (Jeremy Irons), the trickster (Jim Carrey), the princess, the witch, the wise old man, and so on.

For that reason, your screenplays will be stronger if you keep the archetypes at the forefront rather than thinking of specific actors for specific roles.

44| Creating Heroes And Villains Audiences Love

The hero (protagonist) and the villain (antagonist) are the two most important characters in most stories. They have opposing goals and are bound through conflict. Audiences love to see them battle it out. Rooting for a hero with an uphill battle and booing the bad guy is part of the fun of going to the movies.

Protagonist: This is the hero, the main character of your story. These are the essential traits of a compelling protagonist:

- He must be active. He must drive the conflict.
- He must have a strong goal, and he must not compromise.
- He must face a series of ever-increasing obstacles, but he must have some hope of achieving his goal.
- He must be special or unique in a meaningful way.

The audience must empathize with the protagonist. They must root for him. Remember, story is conflict. Nobody wants to watch a hero who doesn't do anything or is indecisive. Make sure he has a goal that he pursues actively. And he must earn his reward. Life shouldn't be too easy for him.

"Make him suffer. Force him to claw his way out," says screenwriter Rose Gumarova. "At first I thought it was sadistic to throw my protagonist into hell. But then I realized that when I'm watching a movie, I love cheering the main character when he's fighting overwhelming opposition. As a writer, if you baby your characters you cheat your audience."

Antagonist: The antagonist wants to stop the hero. Usually the antagonist is another person, but sometimes it's a natural disaster ("*The Day After*"), an animal or a creature ("*Jaws*"), the supernatural ("*The Exorcist*"), or even the character himself battling an inner conflict ("*Leaving Las Vegas*"). Inner conflict, however, is harder to write for the beginning screenwriter.

If you're starting out, build your story around a strong external conflict against a well-defined antagonist. Most antagonists are villains with an unmistakable bad side, but there are exceptions.

In romantic comedies, the protagonist usually ends up marrying the antagonist! Instead of thinking of the antagonist as the bad guy, think of him, her, or it as the main source of opposition to the protagonist. If the protagonist could easily beat the antagonist, there would be no story. No matter how strong the protagonist is, the antagonist must start out stronger, with his own goal that he pursues as rigorously as the protagonist does his.

Develop your antagonist with the same care you devote to your protagonist. Both actors and audiences love a great antagonist. The best villains (Hannibal Lecter, Darth Vader, The Joker) are as complex and interesting as the hero.

45| Dialogue Is Not Conversation

In his book "Story: Substance, Structure, Style and The Principles of Screenwriting," screenwriting expert Robert McKee states that dialogue should have "the swing of everyday talk, but content well above normal."

If I were to transcribe a conversation with my best friend and put it into a screenplay, the audience would fall asleep within seconds. "Yeah, I might go out tonight…Dunno, maybe a movie…" In real life, people ramble, digress, interrupt and repeat themselves. But film dialogue is clear and purposeful. Every word drives the story forward.

Good dialogue conveys a maximum of meaning with a minimum of words. Nevertheless, dialogue still needs to sound like something real people would say. Real people don't speak in full, grammatically perfect sentences or well-composed paragraphs. They use contractions. They drop words. They jump from one thought to another.

Sonny is a nervous bank robber at a bungled hold-up. He's inside the bank with several hostages and Sal, his psychopathic accomplice. Outside, the police have the place surrounded. You may recognize this scenario from *"Dog Day Afternoon"* (written by Frank Pierson) starring a young Al Pacino.

Does Sonny say, "Do you want me to give up? Look, Sal is in the back with the girls. He has his gun pointed at them. If anything should happen to me, Sal will shoot them. If you make one move, the girls will die. How can I be sure you will not jump me?"

No, of course not. This is what Sonny says: SONNY: You want me to give up, huh? Look, Sal's in back with the girls. Anything happens to me--one move--and Sal gives it to them. Boom boom. How do I know you won't jump me?

Remember, "the swing of everyday talk, but content well above normal."

46| Supporting Roles

Most stories have other characters besides the hero and the antagonist. These secondary characters may be part of the main storyline or they may play a role in a subplot. As interesting as these characters and their stories may be in themselves, their importance lies in how they affect the protagonist.

We all interact differently with different people in our lives. You might be lighthearted with your brother, feisty with your boss, and downright homicidal with your in-laws. Just as other people bring out different sides of your personality, supporting characters bring out different sides of the main characters. Someone has to talk sense into a stubborn protagonist, melt the heart of a tough guy, or rile the feathers of a hothead.

We need other characters to push their buttons because that's what creates conflict. Will the protagonist listen to advice, let go of his fear, and embrace love? Or will he resist, fight, and end up alone? Will he overcome his flaw? Or will his flaw get the better of him? Supporting characters allow the story to ask and answer these questions.

If your heroine works double shifts to make ends meet, her boss is important so long as he either hinders or helps her cause. Let's say he keeps hitting on her until she tells him off and gets fired. Then the boss will actually have played a role in her storyline. If, however, the only reason he's there is because employees have bosses and the screenwriter thought it would add some realism to have her chit-chat about the weather with him, then he's dead weight. He should be cut.

Supporting characters are meant to feed the main storyline. The presence of secondary characters should feel organic to the whole. To be believable, they need to come across as characters in their own right without overshadowing the main characters. The more important a supporting character is, the more fully developed he will be.

A major secondary character will not only have his own agenda and defining traits, but possibly his own character arc, too.

47| Talking Heads

One of the biggest mistakes beginning writers make is writing scenes where the characters talk about things that happened rather than showing us the events themselves. Some golden rules of writing merit repetition: show, don't tell!

Avoid talking head scenes by putting your characters in action. If your hero goes to a party, show us the party, not him discussing it over lunch with his friends. If your heroine has a humiliating blind date, show us the date, not the heroine complaining to her girlfriend on the phone. It's okay to have her talk to her girlfriend after the date, but have her say something that gives us new information or subtly shades what we've already seen, like this example from Thelma and Louise.

In a previous scene, we saw J.D. (Brad Pitt) seduce Thelma in a motel room. The following morning, Thelma meets Louise for breakfast. Here's what she tells her best girlfriend about the wild night she spent:

THELMA: Oh my God, Louise!!! I can't believe it! I just really can't believe it! I mean... whoa! I mean I finally understand what all the fuss is about. This is just a whole 'nother ball game!

Notice there's no lengthy description, just how Thelma feels, which adds nuance to what we've already seen. Strengthen your writing by eliminating talking heads scenes and making every word of your dialogue count.

48| Text And Subtext

When my best friend and I talk about our plans for the day, we aren't engaged in serious information exchange. We're more like two birds chirping to each other. Underneath our insignificant words, the real message is: "I care about you. I'm interested in your life." The words are the text, but the meaning, carried by what we're NOT saying, is the subtext. This is how we build relationships in real life. The same concept makes for powerful film dialogue.

The more secure we feel in a relationship, the more likely we are to come out and say what we mean outright. But when things get emotionally risky, we hide our true wants and needs within the subtext. Your characters should do the same. Let's look at some examples.

In this scene from Thelma and Louise, the girls are on the run from the law. Louise is studying a map to find the quickest way to Mexico. It's through Texas, but Louise refuses to take that route. When Thelma asks point blank what happened in Texas, this is how Louise responds:

LOUISE: I just don't think it's the place I wanna get caught for doin' something like...if you blow a guy's head off with his pants down, believe me, Texas is the last place you wanna get caught!

Whatever happened to Louise in Texas is too painful to talk about, so she avoids answering directly.

Here's an example from "*American Beauty*," written by Alan Ball.

Lester (Kevin Spacey) and Carolyn's (Annette Benning) marriage is in trouble. They're on the couch. Lester is drinking a beer. He's frustrated with the materialistic, joyless woman his wife has become. She's furious with him for upsetting her carefully orchestrated balance. He tries to reach the woman she used to be by reminiscing about their early days. She wants to resist but is feeling drawn to the image he paints. They lean toward each other. Will she enter the relationship? Or will she pull away? Just before their lips meet, she says:

CAROLYN: Lester. You're going to spill beer on the couch.

Seemingly banal, her line reveals how ambivalent she really feels about reconnecting with her husband. There are times characters say exactly what they mean, such as at a breaking point moment where the tension finally peaks. If you've done the groundwork and set up the moment, it will seem totally natural, as if the characters can no longer hold back. They've tried to deny the truth, to hide it, or to hint at it—but now they spell it out.

At such moments, text and subtext converge. Use subtext to add layers of meaning, your script will have forward motion, and your characters will always be well-rounded individuals who beg to leap off the page and onto the screen.

49| The Function Of Dialogue

Dialogue needs to accomplish at least one, preferably more, of the following:

- further the plot
- reveal character
- create conflict
- elicit emotion
- deepen our experience of what we see on screen

In the movie "*Some Like it Hot*," written by Billy Wilder and I.A.L. Diamond, Jerry (Jack Lemmon) and Joe (Tony Curtis) are down-and-out musicians who have witnessed a mob hit. Broke and desperate to get out of town alive, they masquerade as women and join a girl's band. Still awkward in their skirts and high heels, they're standing on the platform waiting for a train. Just then, band member Sugar (the ultra-feminine Marilyn Monroe) strolls by carrying her ukulele. Here's what Jerry says:

JERRY: Who are we kidding? Look at that--look how she moves----it's like Jell-O on springs. They must have some sort of a built-in motor. I tell you it's a whole different sex.

This dialogue furthers the plot by foreshadowing the trouble our heroes will have pulling off the masquerade. And, by adding nuance to the images we see on screen, it introduces us to Sugar, a major character. It also exemplifies the conflict of men trying to pass as women, especially in the presence of someone like Sugar, and hints at the additional conflict that's sure to come when two men vie for the attention of one beautiful woman.

The line reveals character, too. We see Jerry's nervousness and his wittiness. We see he's fascinated and intimidated by Sugar. By poking fun at sexuality and identity, this dialogue makes us laugh and sympathize with Jerry and it elicits emotion, too.

If a line of dialogue doesn't further the plot, reveal character, create conflict, elicit emotion, or deepen our experience of what we see on screen, get rid of it. As painful as it can be, all serious writers must develop the discipline to cut any dialogue that doesn't serve the story.

50| What People Say: Dialogue

We've talked a lot about who characters are and what characters do, but what about what characters say?

Let's turn our focus now to dialogue. If you're a movie buff, you'll recognize these lines of dialogue:

"I'll make him an offer he can't refuse."

"Frankly, my dear, I don't give a damn."

"May the Force be with you."

"The Godfather", *"Gone with the Wind"*, and *"Star Wars"* gave us phrases that have entered our collective psyche. Because we love quoting our favorite films, it's tempting to think that good dialogue is the most important part of a movie. But film is a visual medium.

As important as good dialogue is to our understanding and enjoyment of the movie, those lines don't stand alone. What we see gives life to what we hear. I spent several years translating scripts and subtitling films for German companies. My experience taught me that dialogue serves the story and not the other way around. So how does a screenwriter write memorable dialogue that serves the story? By understanding what film dialogue is and isn't.

Completing Your First Draft

51| The "What If?" Question

A good way to brainstorm is by asking, "what if?" Let's say you want to write about a mother and her teenage daughter who are constantly fighting but you're having a hard time coming up with a unique twist to this universal theme. What if their constant bickering spurred someone to cast a spell on them? What if they magically switched bodies? What if the only way to switch back was to learn to understand and accept each other?

This is *"Freaky Friday"* (the 2003 remake). At the heart of every good story lies a "what if?" question. And inside every good writer is a curious child who just won't quit asking, "what if?"

52| Brainstorming

A good way to tap into your creativity is through brainstorming. The idea behind brainstorming is to set a problem and then allow your mind to search for solutions it normally wouldn't come up with.

Set the problem: Start by defining the issue. Do you want to figure out a better setting for your love scene, create a new character, or elevate a line of dialogue? Frame the problem with a question, such as, "How many different ways can Joe insult Terry?" or "Knowing everything I know about Jake, where would he take Susan on a date if he's trying to impress her?" And then allow yourself to come up with answers.

Quantity, not quality: Focus on generating as many ideas as you can without worrying about their quality. In brainstorming, anything goes. Switch off the internal judge, and let the ideas run wild. Write whatever comes to you, no matter how goofy or shocking. Go overboard. You can always throw it away or scale it back later. Only by giving yourself this freedom will you come up with stuff you never dreamed of. Keep at it for as long as you can.

As screenwriter Susannah Farrow puts it, "Brainstorm till it hurts. The first idea you come up with is rarely the best one, the right one, or the most compelling one."

Sometimes it takes one hundred bad ideas to come up with one good one. If you feel awkward at first, it's because you're still judging. It usually takes a minimum of 20 minutes in the beginning before you really shut off your internal critic.

The more you brainstorm, the better you'll get at generating results. Brainstorm with a partner. Sometimes two heads are better than one. Give each other complete freedom to say anything. Once you get all your ideas down, play around with combining them in new and provocative ways.

53| Gathering Ideas

Before we can flesh out a concept, we need an idea that sparks our imagination. Ideas come from the things we experience or are curious about. Feed your creativity—and your soul—by trying new things, meeting new people, and asking lots of questions. Don't turn down an invitation to go parachuting, for example, or to spend a day tracking a paramedic.

A fellow writer once told me that he made opportunities to learn something new each and every day. If he took a cab, he'd interview the cabbie in detail. How long were his shifts? What happened when a customer didn't pay? Had he ever been robbed? He did this even if he wasn't currently writing about a cabbie. He'd simply tuck his notes away for future reference.

Anything, no matter how banal, can serve as a springboard for a story, so become observant in all that you do. Collect ideas every day. Jot down story plots, character descriptions, places you've seen, things you've read about, or snippets of dialogue you've overheard. Try capturing a person's speech pattern and choice of words.

Look up new words you learn. "I like to cut out pictures from magazines," says screenwriter and documentary filmmaker Lindsay Norgard. "This helps me capture a mood or a character."

Always carry paper and pen, a tape recorder, or a camera on you. We absorb so much each day that unless we record it, we'll forget. I use a filing card system so I can separate my notes. For example, if I meet a witty woman at a dinner party, I'll note her snappy dialogue on one card, her physical description on another, and the dinner setting on a third. When I get home, I file my notes under broad categories: plot, dialogue, character, situation, setting, and title. This allows me the freedom to shuffle and combine my ideas as I like, whenever I like.

Each writer has his or her own methods for collecting ideas and brainstorming. Experiment and develop your own. Check out: "The Writer's Idea Book", by Jack Heffron: A book of over 400 prompts and exercises to get the juices flowing.

54| Outlining

Many writers fear wrongly that outlining will stifle their creativity. But in fact, it can lead to amazing breakthroughs. It's much easier to try out wild ideas and test, add, and discard story elements—plot, subplots, characters, and so on—when you're not attached to specific scenes, characters, and lines of dialogue.

Outlining comes after you've developed and tested your concept. Whether you use file cards, a step outline, or another method is up to you, but your outline should include the major events of the story.

In a three-act structure, they would be:

1. Opening scene/s

2. Inciting Incident

3. First turning point at the end of Act I

4. Midpoint

5. Second turning point at the end of Act II

6. Crisis

7. Climax

8. Resolution

On the first run-through, stay focused on the primary story. Include the subplots only when they influence these story events. Then go back and brainstorm connecting scenes and add the subplots.

For example: INT. LAB – NIGHT Hunched over his microscope, David pulls an all-nighter trying to crack the case.

As you work, keep asking questions. Is the central conflict compelling enough to carry the movie? Would the story be better if a different character became the hero? Is the climax powerful?

Go through the outline trying different possibilities. If you get stuck, then you probably need to solidify your central conflict, develop your characters, or do a little research. Take a break from outlining to brainstorm or gather the information you need. You may find your concept shifting as you outline. Don't worry, just take another look at it. Can you improve on it? Once you've elevated your concept, go back to outlining.

55| Do Something Else

You're having a problem with a particular scene or character, and there's no solution in sight. You've spent hours with your butt glued to the chair. You've brainstormed, turned the scene inside out, and even given your character a sex change. Still, nothing. You're beyond frustrated. You're suicidal. Before you hang yourself, consider taking a break. It may sound illogical, but sometimes not working on a problem helps solve it.

Trying too hard to make your brain come up with a solution is like trying to make a small child stop crying by shouting at her—utterly counterproductive. By turning your attention away from the problem, you allow your subconscious to work on it in peace. So give your subconscious a little space, will ya, and go do something else.

Most writers eventually discover which activities coax their creative muse. "My best ideas come when I run and listen to music and really zen out," says screenwriter Lindsay Norgard.

But sometimes the solution just comes to you the same way a name you've had on the tip of your tongue hits you in the middle of folding socks at the Laundromat. Ultimately, it doesn't matter what you do so long as you get away from your story for a while. Sometimes all you'll need are 10 minutes away from your desk. Sometimes you'll need a break of several weeks from a particular scene while you work on something else.

Screenwriting isn't a linear process, so give yourself the time you need. It may seem useless at first, but letting an idea percolate in your subconscious is an essential part of the process.

56| Research

"Write what you know." This is one of the most oft-repeated—and confusing—bits of advice for writers. If what you know is plumbing, does that mean all your characters are doomed to be plumbers forever? I think not.

Hallelujah for research. I like to do the bulk of my research before I begin. I allow myself to follow any tangent, no matter how seemingly irrelevant. I read books I normally wouldn't, and meet people I usually don't run in to. I subscribe to magazines that aren't necessary and Google more than is good for me, all in the name of research. I'm like a sponge, absorbing information, never quite sure how or if I'll use it. Often, your research is not even visible in the script in any direct way. Instead, it seeps into the characters and the story, lending them depth and authenticity.

Research isn't about unfailing accuracy. It's about learning enough to create a cohesive and believable story world. The trick to research is finding the right method and the right balance that works for you.

Too little research, and your story might seem superficial and implausible. Too much research, and you risk turning your script into a litany of facts or procrastinating so much that you don't write altogether.

Research first, then put it away and write. Or write first, and then supplement what you've written with research. Both methods are valid, so use whichever one works best for you.

57| Adaptations And True Stories

Another source of ideas are published novels or incredible true stories. However, unless the novel is in the public domain or the person whose true story you're writing is you, you'll have to secure the rights first. This costs money and is very tricky, but if you're determined, here are some tips from entertainment lawyer Judith Merians:

· Get exclusive rights throughout the universe in all media now known or hereafter invented. Even if you intend to produce only a DVD movie you should buy all media so you don't have competition on the same story in other media.

· If you're getting an option (securing the rights for a limited amount of time, after which they revert back to the original party), get it for a period long enough to pitch, set up a project, and do a draft before the option expires.

· Always get an optional second option period so that if the project is in active development you can extend the option period without having to pay the purchase price. You don't want to have to buy something before you know you're going to produce the project.

· Keep development costs down.

· Do not grant approval rights to the author of the novel or the subject of the life story rights. That can kill a project at the whim of someone who does not want to "approve" for whatever reason. No one will finance this. You can grant consultation rights if the subject insists on being involved.

- Life story rights should cover a broad enough period of the person's life to be able to tell the story. First check to see that you can get the rights to all other real people who are essential to your story. If you can't get the rights to an essential character without whom the story can't be told, and there is not enough information in the public records to write in the character, pass on the project.

- Sign the subject to render exclusive services as a consultant by furnishing photos, documents, interviews, and giving you access to others. Your story will be richer and more authentic, and if anyone else is developing the same story from public records you'll have an edge by having exclusive access to inside information.

- Get everything in a signed document and have all rights documents drafted and negotiated by an experienced lawyer. This is where you spend your money—securing the rights properly.

A warning: many beginning writers try to write their own life experiences. But that horrible breakup you went through at 17 is almost certainly an insufficient story. Creating good drama requires distance. Most of us are too close to our own stories. We get caught up in the personal details and lose sight of the universal. When that happens, the most dramatic event in our lives will only come across as boring to an audience.

58| The Lousy First Draft

Want to make leaps and bounds as a writer? Give yourself permission to write a lousy first draft. Writing and editing are two different processes. How can you feel totally free to be creative and inventive if your inner critic is constantly reading over your shoulder and making faces? Write now, judge later.

Gather your research and decide what a scene is about, then jump in and start writing without worrying about length or word choice or correct spelling or grammar. If you know you need a certain beat here, but it's not coming to you, jot a reminder to yourself to come back to it later and keep going.

After you get your lousy first draft on paper, then refine, elevate, re-arrange, expand, and trim. As screenwriter Andrew Bennett says, "Writers build. Editors cut. You can't do both at the same time."

Here's another trick most writers use: Never show your very rough first draft to anyone. Not your spouse, not your friends, not even your goldfish. It's for your eyes only. Why? Because you never have to worry about anyone's judgment! You can write whatever you want! I didn't show my husband the first draft of this book, and I haven't seen the first draft of his new novel. He may be writing incomprehensible nonsense, but I'll never know. I get to believe he's always brilliant.

If you don't allow yourself the freedom of a lousy first draft, you risk not completing your script. "Always remember the Art of Getting the Damn Thing Done," says Bennett. "Finish your script at all costs. Write an ending that you hate if you can't find a better one right now."

Your subconscious will work on the problem, but only if you give it something to work with. So get it down on paper and trust the process. Embrace the lousy first draft. It's a writer's best friend.

Evaluating Your Screenplay

59| Script Readings

Script readings are a great way to evaluate your script. Hearing your words spoken and seeing your scenes blocked brings your script to life in a way that reading from a page never will.

The simplest way to host a reading is to gather a few friends together. "Do the reading over a few drinks. It's cheap and fun," says screenwriter Andrew Bennett. Try to assign each major character to a different person, but people can double up on the minor roles or the narration. Or consider a public reading.

"I staged a public reading of my script before I attempted to write a new draft," says screenwriter/director Mary V. Dunkerly. "I taped it, which allowed me to review the entire process at my leisure."

Try to find actors to participate. Most screenwriters know at least a couple of actors they can approach. "Actors have fantastic instincts for getting to the essence of things," says director Randa Haines. "When an actor says, 'I don't understand this moment,' that's a terrific help to the writer. It means something needs to be clarified."

One of the biggest advantages of a reading is hearing your dialogue spoken. Does it flow easily, or do the actors struggle with it? Does each character sound distinctive? Is every word essential and does it move the story forward?

"Listening to the actors, I could pinpoint where the dialogue dragged and where it was working," says Dunkerly. Haines also suggests inviting a director to participate. "A director can help a writer move things around. She might look at the staging and suggest putting this scene before that one, or cutting all the dialogue out of another scene and making it purely visual. The actors can try the director's suggestions, and the writer gets to see the scene played out in two, three, or five different ways."

During a reading, refrain from directing or interpreting the action for the readers in any way. Allow everyone to work directly from the script. If their interpretation is wildly different from yours, that's a pretty good indication that the movie in your head isn't coming across on the page.

Stay in observer mode. Take notes, and consider taping the reading. Encourage comments at the end. Write out a questionnaire so that you cover all the bases. Ask questions about your hero's goals, the plotline, and the pacing, and anything else you'd like more information on. A script reading is an eye-opening experience that can transform your writing.

60| Professional Readers

Another source of feedback is the professional script reader. Below, Barb Doyon, professional consultant and owner of Extreme Screenwriting, tells us how to go about it:

"Use a professional consultant before marketing a spec script. The screenwriter is the last person to see shortcomings in his work. A professional consultant offers an objective opinion and helps ready the script for the market. Screenwriters who market scripts before they're ready have greatly affected the way the industry looks at specs. If you want to get beyond the slush pile and be considered a pro, have a professional consultant review your material first.

"Find consultants through word-of-mouth. Ask other screenwriters who they use, and question them to determine if a specific consultant fits your needs. Send the consultant an e-mail asking for referrals. Check out their Web site, if they have one, and look for client testimonials. Have the consultant's clients won or placed in contests, optioned or sold scripts, or secured representation? If a consultant has been in the biz for several years with no track record, then look for someone else. The point is to further your career.

"Don't use friends or family as reviewers. If you have to explain what INT. or EXT. means, then that person shouldn't be reviewing the script. Anyone who knows you personally isn't a candidate for providing an objective review!

"Don't pay money for studio-style coverage, which provides things you already know, like the logline and synopsis, and tends to give vague comments, like the dialogue is too on-the-nose. Instead, find a reviewer who gives story notes. These often include page references so you can spot the problems easily and advice on potential fixes. Both types of review can be useful, but the goal is to help you improve the material and compete on the spec market.

"Don't market a script before it's ready! When a screenwriter finishes a script, it's like a hot potato that he wants out of his hands and onto the market. Slow down! If an idea is really hot, it can wait forever. The spec market is fierce. You're competing with A-list writers, as well as other aspiring screenwriters. Taking the time to make a script the best it can possibly be shows you're a professional.

"Prices for services start around $80-$100 and go up from there depending on the consultant's experience and reputation. Verify any service you're considering before you pay!

Learn More: Barb Doyon offers a free and very informative newsletter for aspiring screenwriters. Sign up through her Web site: http://www.xtremescreenwriting

61| Giving Feedback

Sooner or later you'll be asked to give feedback. This is a great opportunity. Believe it or not, giving feedback will improve your own writing. Giving feedback will teach you what to look for, and searching for solutions to help another writer will train you to solve those same problems for yourself.

When giving feedback, remember the following:

· Keep your comments friendly and encouraging. Critique the writing, not the writer.

· Focus on improving the script, which is helpful, not on improving the writer, which is insulting.

· Look at things from the author's point of view. Try to figure out the story the writer is trying to tell, and keep your comments focused on that.

· Start with the positive. No matter how bad a script is, find something nice to say, even if it's just complimenting the writer for finishing the draft.

· Preceding a negative comment with a positive one softens the blow. Two positives to every negative. Point out parts that are working well as you search for the problems. Keep the ratio as close to two pluses for every minus as possible.

· End with the positive. Close your critique with one last positive, encouraging comment. For positive comments, use the pronoun "you." "The way you got Sally out of that bind was really original." For negative comments, avoid using "you." Instead of saying, "You lost me in the next scene," say "I got confused," or "The next scene was confusing."

· Start with the big picture. If the story isn't working, address those problems first.

· Don't overwhelm the writer with the small stuff. Point out a problem, don't offer a solution. "I'm having a hard time understanding why Joe loves Clara" is helpful. It lets the writer know what is unclear. "I think Joe should be in love with Clara's sister instead" is less helpful. The writer is left to wonder why you feel that way.

· It's okay to point out a problem and then make a suggestion—if you keep your suggestions pertinent and leave plenty of room for the writer to find his own solutions.

· Frame your comments as follows:

- I don't understand who/what/when/where/why/how

- This part feels slow/confusing/redundant…

- I had a hard time following when…

- This scene is very funny/exciting/moving…

- I really empathized with the hero when…

Giving feedback requires attentiveness, thought, and sensitivity. Learn to do this for others—and then apply your new skills to your own script!

62| Receiving Feedback

You've spent months on your script, and now it's time to show it to other people. But what if people hate it? Will you ever live it down? Receiving feedback can be scary at first, but you won't grow as a writer until you plunge in and take this very important step. Don't worry, you'll get the hang of it. Eventually. Take a deep breath, and follow these guidelines:

· Make a distinction between your work and yourself. When someone points out a problem in your script, you don't need to take it to mean there's something wrong with you personally.

· Avoid the temptation to shut down or to argue with the reviewer. Listen to what they have to say without explaining yourself. Remember, you have ultimate control over your script. Only you can decide what works for your script and what doesn't. You don't lose anything by listening. The best response to a review is, "Thank you."

· Listening to others is different from implementing every suggestion. Some reviewers will give you terrific suggestions that fit your story perfectly and take it in the direction you want it to go. Great! Use those. Others will give you terrific suggestions—for a completely different story. Hmm. Skip their suggestions, but do look at your story again to see if it could have possibly led them astray.

· Learn to differentiate between useful suggestions, suggestions that aren't very useful but point to a problem, and totally useless suggestions.

· If the feedback isn't clear, ask questions. Keep the questions pertinent and focused on the work. For example, if the reviewer says, "The scene between George and Becky is confusing," you may want to ask them to explain exactly where in the scene they got confused. Don't ask, "What do you mean it's confusing!?" That sounds defensive and gets everyone off track.

· Avoid asking for feedback if you know what's wrong with your script. Fix any problems you are clear about first. When you ask for feedback, you're requesting someone's time and attention, so be considerate of them.

· Don't make them do unnecessary work. Pay special attention to problems that multiple readers point out. If only one person out of several readers had a problem, you can probably ignore it. But if several readers bring up the same issue, then be sure to address it.

Concentrate on your screenplays and the clarity of your vision. In time, you'll learn to attach ever less importance to other people's opinions.

63| Your Trusted Circle Of Readers

No writer should be without a trusted circle of readers. You need to surround yourself with clear-thinking readers who are willing and able to give candid feedback.

"Find and keep very dear anyone who tells it like it is," says writer/director Joy Perino. "Honest—not mean or fawning—feedback is precious and very hard to come by."

If you're taking a screenwriting class and there's a classmate whose work you admire, suggest an exchange. Approach a former writing instructor you've stayed in contact with. Or consider joining a local critiquing group. If you can't find a group in your area, consider joining one online. A few precautions, however:

· Avoid critique groups that only tell you how wonderful you are, as well as the ones where everyone tears everyone else down. Both types exist. Neither approach is helpful.

· Join a working group, not a social club. Make sure there's a submission schedule and a minimum critiquing requirement, and that the group actually sticks to it.

Building your trusted circle of readers takes time, but once you do, you won't know how you ever lived without those precious people. Don't forget to them in your Oscar acceptance speech.

The Rewriting Phase

64| Getting Dirty

Think of your first draft as a lump of clay: malleable, flexible raw material. To mold it into a solid screenplay, you need to feel totally free to add, subtract, rearrange, destroy, and reshape material. Jump in, get dirty up to the elbows, allow yourself to feel the grit under your fingernails. Rewriting isn't a job for sissies.

The biggest mistake you could make in the rewriting phase is to get too precious with your first draft. Don't be afraid of losing material you like. If it doesn't fit the story, be disciplined enough to throw it out. This is known as "killing your darlings," and it's an essential skill to develop. As screenwriter Andrew Bennett put it, "Great writers aren't great first-drafters. They're great rewriters." You may be head over heels in love with your first draft, and maybe it even deserves all that affection. But once you have rewritten a script several times, take your final draft and compare it with the first one. Most writers will admit that their brilliant first draft now appears terribly flawed and downright unlovable. So save a copy of your current draft in a read-only file if it makes you feel better. Then roll up your sleeves and let the mudslinging begin.

65| Fix The Story Problems

Too many writers seem to believe rewriting means tinkering with the small stuff—lines of dialogue, finding the perfect adjective, fiddling with spelling and grammar. While that is definitely a part of rewriting, it's not the place to start. Concentrate on the big picture. Make sure your story works. You might have to cut or add scenes or characters, rewrite your entire opening or ending, or even rethink your entire concept. So why spend time perfecting something you might end up throwing out?

Write a one-page synopsis of your story. Use one paragraph for each act. Is the synopsis exciting? Does the story hold together? If not, perfect the synopsis and use it as a guide for your rewrite. Here are some points to keep in mind when analyzing your story for weaknesses:

• Reexamine your central conflict. Is it as powerful as it can be?

• What is the ultimate story question? Has it been answered?

• What is the story's theme? Can you articulate it?

- Does your story stay on track, or does it meander?

- Does your story have organic turning points (inciting incident, act climaxes)?

- Does your hero face ever more difficult obstacles? Does the plot build momentum?

- Is your hero the best hero for this story? Is his goal clear, does he drive the story, and does he have a character arc?

- What about the antagonist? Is he the best antagonist for this story?

- Are there any plot holes?

- Are the subplots working? Do they contribute to the story by supporting or contrasting the main theme?

- Does the story have an ebb and flow of tension that keeps the audience permanently interested?

66| Smooth Out Your Scenes

Does every scene in your script have a purpose? Does the scene move the story forward? Or is a scene there simply to entertain or to shade the character a little? Unneeded scenes waste precious time. Go through your script and look for flabby or redundant scenes and either rewrite or cut them. Once you've decided a scene is necessary, make it the best it can be. Here are some questions to guide you:

· Is there a dramatically compelling conflict and goal in this scene?

· Do you have the right characters for this scene?

· Do we know who drives the scene?

· Does the character succeed or fail in achieving his goal?

· Does the scene start and end at the right places?

· Is the setting the best possible setting?

· Are the actions visually compelling and in character?

· Does the scene have a beginning, middle, and end?

Do the same for your scene sequences:

· Do the complications get progressively harder?

· Do they build to a turning point?

· Do the scenes flow naturally and logically?

67| Solidify Your Characters

Are you having trouble making your hero likable? You probably need to work on his setup. Remember the golden rule: Show, don't tell. Repeat for every major character. Here are some more points to keep in mind during the rewrite:

• Do your characters have clear agendas and goals? Is their primary conflict external?

• Does every character in the script have a story purpose? Are they the best characters for this story?

• Do you have two characters that are too similar? If so, can you eliminate one or combine them into a single character?

• Have you given your characters an inner conflict and a character flaw?

• Are your characters drawn into relationship through rapport and conflict?

• Do all major characters have a character arc?

• Are your hero and antagonist introduced in a compelling and dramatically exciting way?

Try the following exercise. Create a mind map of conflict. Write down the name of your hero, his antagonist(s), and every substantial secondary character. Then draw arrows indicating who is in conflict with whom, and over what. If any one character is left without an arrow pointing directly or indirectly to your hero, he or she is a hindrance to your script. Even your hero's best friend ought to disagree with him at some point.

68| Punch Up The Dialogue

Now that you've worked through your story problems and have solidified your characters, you can turn your attention to dialogue. It's normal to have a lot of on-the-nose dialogue in a first draft. But now it's time to punch it up. Does your dialogue:

• propel the action forward by anticipating the future through predictions, warnings, or implication?

• deliver emotion (funny, threatening, evasive)?

• come from your character's core traits?

• have subtext?

• allow for moments of wordless communication, such as silence itself or action in place of words?

• use metaphor, irony, and sarcasm?

• generate unexpected responses?

• go to the extreme?

• contain jargon?

Remember, good dialogue is a match of wills. Depending on your story and characters, the tussle of words can be fun and playful. Put your characters in situations of constantly negotiating their status, and your dialogue will come to life.

69| Eliminate Clichès

Clichés are ideas, thoughts, phrases, and metaphors that were once original and insightful but have now lost both insight and originality and have become empty and formulaic. Earlier I mentioned an example of a once-original twist that is now a plot clichés the corrupt cop as criminal. But clichés can appear just about anywhere—in your concept, your plot, your characters, your dialogue, even in the screenwriting devices you use. Examples of clichés in everyday speech are phrases such as, "at the end of the day," "I gave him the best years of my life," and even "all's well that ends well," which wasn't a cliché when Shakespeare penned it.

Go through your script one more time and sniff out cliché formulas, gimmicks, and anything that is overused and misused. For example, if you want to show the passage of time, think of a more interesting way than cutting to a clock. Examine your scene transitions, your character responses, and the devices you use to create anticipation. Make sure they're varied and fresh. "Devices should help you create unpredictable characters and situations," says screenwriter/editor Jackie Pike. "But used too frequently, they turn into clichés. Amateurs use one device four hundred times. Great writers use four hundred different devices."

Eliminating clichés means never being satisfied with the first idea that comes to mind. No matter how much work it takes, if you become relentless in stamping out clichés your script will improve dramatically.

70| The Final Edit

Congratulations! You started with the big picture. You worked your way through story and character problems, you elevated your dialogue, and you got rid of clichés. Now, finally, is the moment you've been waiting for: agonizing over every single word. A few tricks of the trade:

Choose the most descriptive verb. John sees his girlfriend flirting with another man at the bar. Does he simply walk over? Or does he march, sidle, or sneak up?

Eliminate adverbs. Adverbs modify a verb and they usually end in "ly." Some examples are "answers quietly," "sits heavily," and "runs quickly." Adverbs tell how someone did something. If your scene is well written, if you've shown rather than told, adverbs become superfluous. Show us "sitting heavily" with a more descriptive verb—plop, collapse. Ditto for "answers quietly" (whispers) and "runs quickly" (races).

Use specific nouns. Replace say-nothing, generic nouns with more descriptive ones. Is it a house? Or is it a mansion, a hut, or a dump? Does your hero drive a car? Or does he drive a station wagon, a pick-up, or a convertible? Descriptive nouns imply different things. A character who lives in a house and drives a car tells us nothing, but put him in a mansion and give him a pick-up truck, and you paint a specific picture.

Use specific nouns. Replace say-nothing, generic nouns with more descriptive ones. Is it a house? Or is it a mansion, a hut, or a dump? Does your hero drive a car? Or does he drive a station wagon, a pick-up, or a convertible? Descriptive nouns imply different things. A character who lives in a house and drives a car tells us nothing, but put him in a mansion and give him a pick-up truck, and you paint a specific picture.

Cut down on adjectives. Adjectives describe nouns: a big man, a comfortable chair. Like adverbs, most adjectives are superfluous and can be eliminated. For example, an expensive Rolex is redundant, since all Rolexes are expensive. Sometimes you can bypass an adjective by choosing a more descriptive noun. Thus a big man becomes a colossus, and a comfortable chair becomes a recliner. There are times, however, to use adjectives, and that's when they add something new or unexpected. If you write about a melancholy bride, for example, we perk up. Why? Brides are supposed to be happy, so we wonder why this one is not. Choose your adjectives carefully. Only use them if they're necessary and add something to your script.

End with a punch. Create forward momentum by leaving the punch line for the end. Suppose your teenaged hero says: "I'm going to save my Mom. Because I'll have to live with it forever if I don't." Now flip it: "I'm going to save my Mom. Because if I don't, I'll have to live with it forever." Saving the most important word (forever) for last stops you from giving the joke away too soon and keeps the reader involved until the end.

Check spelling, grammar, and formatting when everything else is done. Have someone else proofread your script.

71| Is It Done, Yet?

In some ways, a script is never done. If you pick up a script today that you thought you finished a year ago, I bet you'll find things to change. But at some point you have to decide it's time to send it out.

Ask yourself, "Can it be better?" If you can honestly answer, "Not to the best of my knowledge," then submit it somewhere. If you have turned yourself inside out, fixed every problem you saw, put the script aside, looked at it again and again, and satisfied yourself that you've done your best, kiss your script goodbye and send it to fend for itself in the wilds of Hollywood. Most likely it'll come home with its tail between its legs, begging you for another rewrite, but don't despair. Take your lumps with pride and pat yourself on the shoulder for having made the next step. Your choices are either to rewrite it yet again or to start a new screenplay.

Unfortunately, most screenwriters send their script out when their answer to "Can it be better?" is, "No. It's perfect! Except for that little problem in the second act. And I still haven't resolved the love story. But otherwise it's ready." Don't make this mistake. Be honest with yourself when evaluating your work. If you see a problem, others will, too. No matter how sick you are of working on the damned thing or how eager for market feedback, never, ever market a script you know is flawed. Find the discipline to finish the job.

Marketing Your Screenplay

72| Agents Make Money FOR You, Not OFF You

An agent only makes money AFTER he's procured work for you—through a sale, option, or writing assignment. Then, and only then, is he allowed to charge you a 10% fee. Legitimate agents who are looking for new clients will never ask you for money. It's against the WGA signatory rules—another good reason to stick with WGA signatory agents.

There are unscrupulous people who use the Internet to seduce inexperienced writers with promises of representation, and then try to charge a reading fee or sell script doctoring services. Don't fall for this.

Bottom line: never, ever pay an agent to read your script or to represent you.

73| Agents, Manager, And Lawyers-Oh, My!

These days, writers are often told they need an agent *and* a manager *and* an entertainment lawyer. What do each of these professionals do? And when do you need whom? For answers, I turned to entertainment lawyer Judith Merians:

"An agent gets your material to buyers. He can also try to get you hired for writing assignments. An agent is only as good as his belief in you and his contacts in the industry. He has to be able to get your material read by the people who can get projects developed and financed. Most companies will only take submissions from agents or entertainment attorneys because unsolicited scripts often lead to lawsuits.

"Agents only make money if you make money since they work on commission. If you're unknown, they'll have to work very hard to get your material read. Most would rather spend their time with clients whose material they can sell more easily.

"Getting your first agent is a challenge. If you can get a recommendation from a client or friend of theirs, they might represent you on a single project. If it sells, then they may take you on as a client.

"A manager sets up meetings for you, gets you known, even helps you find an agent. Managers are prohibited by law from making deals and sales, although this is often ignored. A manager has to be well connected because their fundamental job is to get you well connected. Many managers also help you hone your writing and steer your career.

"Like agents, managers will only take you on if they feel they can make money from you. If you've won awards or have been recognized in some significant way, use your success to interest an agent or manager.

"An entertainment lawyer makes your deal, gets you the best terms, and protects you. A good attorney will know what deals are being made, how much to ask for, and what other rights you should secure—like the right to do one or two rewrites, sequels, or spin-offs.

"Writers should never negotiate deals themselves. They may overlook lots of important points and cause antagonism with the person hiring them. Negotiating is an adversarial process. As a writer, you want to maintain a good relationship with your producer at all times. Let your attorney or agent act like a tough cookie on your behalf.

"Once you have representation, continue marketing yourself. Your agent probably has dozens of clients. If you really want your career to move forward, you'll have to prove you're worth his time. Be proactive. Keep networking. Send him leads. Be grateful for every commission he earns while working for you—including on leads you've initiated yourself. Remember, he works very hard at building his reputation and establishing connections. A phone call from him gets you in the very doors you couldn't open by yourself. Concentrate on being a good client. Do quality work and be reliable."

74| Breaking Into Hollywood

Hundreds of thousands of scripts are written and shopped around, but only about 400 feature films are produced in Hollywood each year. The competition is fierce, so how does a novice screenwriter break in?

According to producer/manager Hal Croasmun, there are numerous routes into Hollywood. "Too many screenwriters give up after trying only the traditional strategies," says Croasmun of ScriptForSale.com. "We didn't want to see any more dreams die over a lack of options." That's why Croasmun, who is also a writer, developed the free program "33 Ways to Break Into Hollywood." Every other day, a new strategy pops up on your desktop until you've read all 33 strategies. It's designed to give you time to consider each tip carefully. Once you've read a strategy, you can review it again at any time. You'll learn how to win contests with industry recognition (strategy #5), approach indie filmmakers (strategy #17), and build your Web site (strategy #10). By the time you've finished, you'll be able to put together an amazing marketing campaign that will get you noticed by Hollywood.

This tool is one of my favorites. No writer should be without it. 33 Strategies can be downloaded for free at http://www.scriptforsale.com/33ways/signup33.htm

75| Contests

Screenwriting contests can be a good way to get exposure, but you need to be smart about how you go about it. Contest entry fees are expensive. Take the time to do your research, be selective, and watch out for scams. The two granddaddies of screenwriting contests are the Walt Disney Screenwriting Fellowship and the Nicholl Fellowship. Winning Disney will get you a $50,000 stipend and a year working and learning at Disney. Placing or winning Nicholl also lands you a large cash prize and plenty of attention from agents. Other contests - no matter how large the payout - pale in comparison. Winning a less prestigious contest can be a good thing on your resume—if you know how to exploit it.

"If you win first place, shout it from the mountaintops," says screenwriter Andrew Bennett. Industry pros will be more willing to look at a winning script, but be ready to strike while the iron is hot and before the next contest announces a fresh batch of winners. "If you placed second in a competition, you still 'won.' If you were a quarterfinalist, you 'placed highly.' The issue is building credibility," says Bennett. There are three strategies to entering contests.

1. Enter to get industry recognition. Seek out contests with industry players as judges, or ones that announce the winners in Variety or The Hollywood Reporter. If this is your aim, write high-concept scripts.

2. Use contests as a sounding board, just to see what kind of resonance you get. Choose contests that offer feedback, so at least this way you get something back for your entry fee.

3. Enter contests with big cash prizes and enter to win. It's a long shot, but if you enjoy that sort of thing, why not? Motivation is the name of the game.

The biggest problem with contests is that too often, the winning scripts don't accurately reflect projects that Hollywood actually wants. Contest judges aren't investing cold, hard cash in the projects they select, so they can allow themselves the freedom of choosing a script they love, no matter how unmarketable. Take contest wins and placements for what they are: confirmation that your writing talent has placed you somewhere in the ballpark. It doesn't necessarily mean you're home free.

Walt Disney Screenwriting Fellowship:
http://www.abctalentdevelopment.com/html/writing_fellowship_mainpage.htm

Nicholl Fellowship in Screenwriting:
http://www.oscars.org/nicholl/ Find other contest listings at http://www.moviebytes.com

76| Getting Past The Gatekeeper: The Reader

When you submit your script to a production company, it'll be evaluated by a reader. Readers are usually young people trying to break into the industry. More often than not, they're freelancers working for about $50 a script. They're stressed. They read tons of scripts, and they read them fast. It doesn't take them long to get pretty good at separating the wheat from the chaff.

The reader is the first person to see your script. He acts as a gatekeeper between you and his boss. His job is to "cover" your script by writing a two-page summary, rating the different story elements, and checking one of three essential boxes: PASS, CONSIDER, or RECOMMEND. If he checks PASS, that's it. Your script is rejected. If he checks CONSIDER or RECOMMEND, then your script goes to his boss, who will evaluate it for himself. The majority of scripts rank no better than PASS.

So how do you get an overworked, underpaid reader to recommend your script? By delivering a professional, well-written, original script. Here are some things to keep in mind:

• Turn in a flawlessly formatted script with lots of white space. Respect the page count.

• Deliver a good, lean story and a satisfying emotional experience.

• Be clear in your writing, but never dumb it down. The reader isn't stupid.

- Grab the reader's attention on page one, and keep grabbing it on every page.

- Establish the central conflict by page 10.

- Create characters we care about with goals we root for.

- Keep increasing the stakes throughout the script.

- Deliver a surprising but inevitable ending.

- Wrap up (resolve) loose ends in five pages or less.

- Write with confidence and hone your style.

Adhere to these guidelines and your script will stand out as professional. Even if a reader passes, at least he'll remember you fondly.

77| Loglines

When you pitch a busy studio executive, he only wants to know two things: What's your story about and is there a potential movie? A powerful logline gets your concept across clearly and concisely and answers both questions in a nanosecond.

Loglines are an important marketing tool. You can use them on your query letters, at pitch fests, even in social situations. But did you know loglines are also an important writer's tool?

Your logline is your GPS system. Write it before you start your script and tape it up where you can see it. A good logline clarifies your concept and keeps you on track as you write. If you wander off path, a glance at the logline steers you back. It's okay to rewrite your logline as your story evolves, but it's not okay to neglect your logline and follow a story that is derailing. Your logline's first duty is to hook us in a few words.

"The true story about the first female pilot" is a good hook. It gives us what's special about the movie—the first woman pilot—and we can begin to see a movie. But we're not done yet. Without worrying too much about details at first, sketch out your logline in a hero-goal-obstacle format:

"This is a story about _____ (the hero) who wants _____ (the goal) but can't have it / do it because _____(the obstacle)."

"This is the story about a guy who wants to star in Broadway musicals but finds he doesn't have what it takes."

LifeTips.com > > Marketing Your Screenplay

Now turn to the details. The above logline is vague. It doesn't spark the imagination. Who is this guy? What doesn't he have? What kind of movie is this (drama, comedy)?

Be specific: "A guy wants to star in Broadway musicals but he can't sing." Okay, at least now we know the problem. But it's still not crystal-clear. We still don't really see the hero or know the genre. No producer will plunk down money for this.

Let's give the logline some attention-grabbing adjectives and nouns: "A wanna-be Broadway singer with tons of stage presence but no voice lip-synchs his way through a starring role and becomes an overnight sensation." Now we can see the hero, the problem, and even the genre (most likely comedy).

The questions being generated are story questions: How did he finagle his way into lip-synching? Will he be revealed as a fraud? Will he learn to sing? Don't you want to write the damned thing just to find out? With any luck, the producer will request your script to find out, too. There's much more to loglines than I can cover here. Begin by reading movie descriptions in TV Guide and writing loglines for movies you've seen.

78| Los Angeles Or Bust?

Do you have to live in L.A. to make it as a screenwriter? If you're writing for TV, living in L.A. is not an option, it's a must. But feature writers have some leeway. "You don't have to be in N.Y. or L.A. to sell a script if you understand the importance of targeting the buyers make the kinds of films that you're writing," says entertainment lawyer Judith Merians.

Certainly, there are advantages to living in L.A. On the one hand, you're in the thick of things. You can get an industry job. If you're lucky enough to land an agent, you can take meetings at a moment's notice. On the other hand, all that networking might distract you from your writing, which isn't a good thing.

The decision to move or not to move to L.A. depends on your personality. Move to L.A. and you may go crazy with the city's demands; don't move there and you may have to work twice as hard to get a career going. "Even if you don't live in Hollywood, get out to L.A. once in a while. Meeting other writers and attending industry events give you a chance to make new contacts," says screenwriter/director Mary V. Dunkerly.

If you decide to make the big move, prepare well in advance. Arrive with a handful of polished scripts and a budget. Make a realistic strategy, akin to a business plan, for what you want to accomplish during your first year.

"If you come to Hollywood, expect to work harder than you ever have before," says screenwriter Andrew Bennett. "Prepare yourself to be a lonely grain of sand in a sea of others just like you. Stay positive. Network and cultivate contacts. Above all, don't quit. I'd like to tell you it gets easier, but I don't want to lie. But it gets easier to tell yourself that it'll get easier soon."

Learn More: Michael Lent's book, Breakfast with Sharks, is a thorough study of becoming a working writer in L.A.

79| Pitching

A pitch is a brief, verbal summary of your story. Like the synopsis, a pitch should focus on selling rather than telling the story. Your goal is to excite the producer about your story and inspire him to request the script.

Start with your logline, and continue with the most original and interesting aspects of your script. Give a clear picture of the beginning, middle, and end. The producer needs to understand your story, so don't be cagy. Know your story and characters inside and out, and be ready with detailed answers to any questions the producer may have. But don't give more away than he asks for. If the producer requests the script after the logline, stop talking! The pitch has done its job, so quit while you're ahead.

You may be stopped after your logline with a polite, "thanks but it's not for us," or you may be asked to continue, so practice talking about your story for two minutes, five minutes, and longer. Rehearse until you can rattle it off in a relaxed and clear manner. Pitch to family and friends and ask for feedback. Was anything confusing? Were they bored? Hone your pitch based on their comments.

Pitching is a performance requiring enthusiasm and humor. Be passionate about your story. Maintain eye contact, engage your listener, and be aware of your body language.

Screenwriter/director Mary V. Dunkerly says the best advice she ever got was to reveal the inspiration for her story before going into the pitch. People love an entertaining behind-the-creative-process story. "During one pitch, I had the listener in stitches telling him about my older friend's first wedding and the Las Vegas-type nuptials she was planning, and how that inspired the story I wrote. Needless to say, he requested the script," says Dunkerly.

At the end of the meeting, don't overstay your welcome. Even if the producer isn't interested, remember you're selling yourself as much as your script, so be friendly, thank him for his time, and get out of there. Leave him with the impression that you're cool, composed, and professional, and he'll be more willing to meet with you again.

80| Pitch Fests

You might want to attend a pitch fest, an organized event that brings aspiring writers face-to-face with industry executives. A pitch fest can be a wonderful experience, especially if it allows you to give multiple pitches. Okay, so it may not feel wonderful the first time around, but the more you practice your pitch, the better you'll get at it—and that does feel pretty good. You'll be exposed to industry professionals, and there may even be workshops for you to attend. Before you sign up for one, however, think through the following:

· Pitch fests can be expensive, especially if you have to travel to L.A., so confirm what you're getting for your money before you go. Some pitch fests make you pay every time you pitch. Others offer package deals. Set your budget in advance.

· Ask about the schedule. How often will you have the opportunity to pitch? Whom will you be pitching to? Will there be pitching workshops where you can get feedback on how you're doing?

· Pitch fests attract huge crowds. The experience has been likened to speed dating, and can be hectic and overwhelming—or exciting and energizing, depending on your personality. Be sure to ask how many attendees are expected.

· Don't get scammed. Check credentials before you sign up for anything. How long has the pitch fest been around? Who will be there? Be wary of pitch fests that keep changing dates or organizers who don't e-mail you back. If in doubt, don't sign up.

· Don't worry about the results. If you attend a pitch fest, don't go expecting to sell your script. Instead, concentrate on gaining pitching experience and building relationships. Maybe a producer didn't request your script, but if you made a good impression, he might be happy to read your next query letter. Look at pitch fests as a networking opportunity and a necessary part of your education, and you won't be disappointed.

Check Out:

Great American Pitch Fest
(http://www.pitchfest.com)

Hollywood Pitch Festival
(http://www.fadeinonline.com/events)

Screenwriting Expo
(http://www.screenwritingexpo.com)

81| Protect Your Work

While plagiarism happens and is therefore a concern, it's a minor one. A legitimate agent or producer won't steal your work. If he's interested in your script, it's easier to pay you than to re-invent it himself. Besides, litigation is expensive, and his reputation is at stake. Follow these guidelines to protect both you and the people you pitch to:

· Register your script with the US Copyright Office and the Writers Guild of America (WGA). Reputable agents, producers, and competitions will strongly recommend or even insist you register your script before showing it to them. While registration doesn't prevent plagiarism, it does provide you with legal proof of the material's existence. If you go to court, the WGA can testify to that evidence.

· Be selective of whom you pitch to. Try to find out a little bit about each person seeing your script. Work only with agents who are WGA signatories. A WGA-signatory agent is bound to abide by the WGA's rules, written to protect the writer. You'll find a list at http://www.wga.org.

· Keep all notes, drafts, and correspondence about your script, from scribbles on a napkin to the finished product. Create a paper trail that proves you are the author of the script.

· Establish a clear business relationship. If vague promises are made, follow up in writing ASAP confirming the agreement as you understood it.

· Finally, keep in mind that ideas and storylines can't be protected. Only your script falls under protection.

82| Query Letters

A one-page query letter sums up your project and asks (queries) the recipient (usually an agent or producer) if he'd like to see the script. Some writers believe query letters are too hit-and-miss and usually thrown away unread, and therefore a waste of time. They prefer to concentrate on getting referrals and making connections. There's a great deal of validity to this point of view. Other writers, however, have had success with queries. It's still good to know how to write one for when you do eventually make a contact. The tips below come from screenwriter Andrew Bennett, who credits the writer Paul Lawrence with them. They can be used for e-mail, fax, and snail mail queries. They showcase your professionalism and increase the likelihood of a positive response.

• Start with a quote about yourself from someone who matters—contest judge, producer, working writer, director.

• Always find the exact name, spelled correctly, of the person you're contacting.

• Open with a brief introduction.

• Follow with your highest element of credibility. This could be a contest win, good coverage, a script of yours that was optioned or is in production, or even any special expertise that you may have. If your script is about the first brain transplant and you're a brain surgeon, you'll come across as credible.

- Deliver the logline for your script. If it's a great high concept, all the better.

- Follow it with a very brief synopsis containing the bare-bones elements of your story: two or three short paragraphs delivering the essentials about your protagonist, his conflict, and each of the major plot points (Act I and II breaks).

- Tell or at least imply the ending in a way that is compelling and inspires a producer to want to read the script.

- Be clear about what you want. I simply ask "May I send you the script?"

- Include contact info.

- Paste a resume at the end.

- For e-mails, use the subject line: From the Office of (Your Name).

83| Synopsis

A synopsis is a brief summary of your story. Depending on whom you talk to, the length of a synopsis might range from a single paragraph to two or three pages, so if you're asked for a synopsis, clarify exactly what the person is looking for. For our purposes here, we'll discuss a very brief synopsis of three to five short paragraphs that you can include in query letters.

A synopsis is a selling tool. "Telling your story is different from selling your story," says producer Hal Croasmun. "Take off the 'screenwriting' hat and put on the 'marketing' hat. Your objective is to hook producers into demanding your script." Here are some tips for writing a persuasive synopsis:

· Place your logline at the top of the page. Then skip a line or two and begin the synopsis.

· Be brief. Limit yourself to a line or two of introduction, one paragraph of three to five lines per act, and one line of conclusion.

· Find the hook. What makes your story different? Build your synopsis around the most original aspect of your story.

· Tell your story chronologically from start to finish. Define the protagonist, the problem, the antagonist, and hint at a conclusion. Skip any details that don't directly contribute to the central conflict, but include all major characters and events, important twists, and the ending.

· Lead with a catchy or provocative opening.

The same principles that apply to screenwriting apply here as well: Grab 'em early. And keep grabbing 'em every step of the way. Echo the genre and tone of your script. Don't tell us "This is a comedy about...," or "In this action-packed thriller... ." Instead, write the synopsis itself in a way that is funny or thrilling.

A synopsis reflects your ability as a writer. Take the opportunity to impress the reader with your writing style. Write visually. Use image-specific words ("hut" instead of "house"). Help the reader see the movie as you see it. Use present tense, strong verbs and nouns, and limit your adjectives and adverbs. Be precise. Don't confuse lack of clarity with mystique. Instead of writing "John discovers something that will change his life forever," tell us "John discovers the time-travel machine." Precision keeps the reader involved.

Get feedback on your synopsis from friends and especially other writers. Write as many drafts as you need to until you get it right. A cohesive, well-written synopsis will get your script requested. A mediocre one will only land in the garbage.

84| The First Rules Of Marketing

People with artistic and creative sensibilities sometimes are handicapped by a lack of business savvy. They love holing up in a turret and writing masterpieces by candlelight, but when it comes to selling their work, they freeze up and die. But marketing is like any other skill: it can be developed over time.

The worst sin you can commit in Hollywood, the world capital of entertainment, is to be boring. Make sure your script is original and entertaining. Give us vivid characters we can love. Give us a conflict we can root for. And then write your marketing materials with the same level of excitement and enthusiasm.

If you've written a comedy, your synopsis should be funny. If you've written a thriller, your logline needs to thrill. When pitching, infect your listeners with your passion. If you're not excited by your script, how will anyone else ever be?

Writing synopses, loglines, query letters and e-mails; pitching scripts and concepts verbally, one-on-one or in front of a group; and projecting a glow of confidence and accomplishment are all part of a screenwriter's life. You need to hone these skills with the same care you devote to your storylines and your characters.

85| The Global Perspective

The film industry is becoming ever more global. Many countries have thriving movie cultures, such as France, India, and upstarts like New Zealand, where Peter Jackson's success ("*The Lord of the Rings*", "*King Kong*") has anchored a burgeoning industry. If you're broadminded and proactive, you may well find riches far from L.A.

One organization, DreamAgo, helps nurture screenwriters and develop their projects for the screen. Founded in France in 2005 and run by screenwriter/consultant Pascale Rey, DreamAgo is a nonprofit organization with branches in Paris, Los Angeles, Madrid, and Lausanne. "The cornerstone of each and every movie is the script," says Rey, DreamAgo's president. "Our goal is to help writers turn their scripts into strong, personal, emotional movies with wide and diverse audience appeal. Our mission is to bring screenwriters, directors, producers and distributors of all nationalities together."

DreamAgo offers an international forum for professional networking and exchange through monthly luncheons and other events such as screenings and meetings. In addition, DreamAgo organizes screenwriting master classes and workshops (including a one-week retreat in Switzerland), and offers a script translation service. DreamAgo works at building contacts with respected artists from all over the world.

To date, its patrons, who act as artistic references and advisors and provide moral support, include Stephen Frears (UK), Alain Corneau (France), Jose F. Lacaba (Philippines), Jorge Perugorria (Cuba), and Guillermo Arriaga (Mexico). If you're interested in applying for membership, visit DreamAgo's Web site: http://www.dreamago.com.

Alternatively, check out film and screenwriting organizations in your country, as well as the home page of the **International Affiliation of Writers Guilds** (http://www.iawg.org), where you'll find links to guilds all over the world. Go to each site and explore its links in turn, and you'll begin to get a sense of what's happening globally.

86| The Indie Scene

Most screenwriters concentrate their efforts on selling to the studios. But what about checking out the indie market? Independent filmmakers need scripts, too, and it just might be an easier market to break into.

"The indie scene offers opportunities for stories that aren't mainline, happy ending, franchise constructed, star vehicles," says entertainment lawyer Judith Merians. "If you have such a story, focus on pitching to producers or production companies who have succeeded with independent films and who have access to money. Look up which companies have deals with the majors and can knock at the doors of their home studios and pitch your project. Also look to directors who like offbeat stories and actors who like stretching their range (Edward Norton, Harvey Keitel, Toni Collette, and the like). Do your homework. Sometimes talent has its own production shingle."

When you have a mainstream high concept that is strong enough to attract stars and carry the movie based on the idea alone, you may have some wiggle room in your writing.

In the indie market, it's not the idea that rules, it's the execution. Your character-driven script lives or dies based on its quality. Be prepared to show a writing sample, and to work on spec and do rewrites. Deliver the script they want. Remember, you're looking for your big break, so keep your nose to the grindstone and your inner prima donna in check.

How to Find Independent Filmmakers:

· Look up housekeeping deals in The Hollywood Directory.

· The International Movie Database (http://www.imdb.com) is a great resource. Look up your favorite indie films. At the bottom of the cast list, click "more." Scroll down to "produced by," and you'll know exactly who produced the movie—and might be interested in your story.

· Check out http://hollywoodlitsales.com.

· Attend film festivals.

· Contact your local film association.

87| Writing For TV

Writing for television is different from writing feature films. "TV is a writer's medium," says producer Harry Waterson (*Soap, Benson, The Golden Girls*). "In episodic television, the writers run the production and the director is mostly just a hired hand. Features are a director's medium and the writer is the hired hand. Witness how many feature writers want to direct so they can have a say in how their script is produced."

Besides talent, what does an aspiring TV writer need? "Speed, smarts, a thick hide, and the ability to write and rewrite as part of a group," says Waterson. He explains further:

Speed: Episodic television is a constant stream of deadlines generating rewrite after rewrite. Locking the script is usually an unfulfilled dream.

Smarts: The episodic TV writer works on as many as half a dozen scripts at a time in various stages of prep or production. He needs to keep all of this straight in his head and to foresee the production traps his writing will generate.

A thick hide: The episodic TV writer has to accept that nothing is written in stone. The rewrite he has just slaved over is immediately given to another staff writer to fix. Or the actor who reads his dialogue doesn't understand it and therefore hates it and wants it rewritten. This has to be done for a run-through two hours from now.

Writing and rewriting as part of a group: Writing is normally a solitary game. Not in episodic television. Talent is very scarce. Writers who can do it all are even rarer. So there are writers who are good at dialogue, good at joke, good at plot construction, good at springboards, or just good at keeping everybody in the room happy. It's the head writer and/or show runner who keeps all these writers on his staff rubbing along together and getting shows done.

How does a new writer break in? "When a series first goes on the air, there is no backlog of material and the writers are still finding their way," says Waterson. "They're living from hand to mouth. The head writer is going nuts with writers who aren't delivering his vision. He's on the phone daily to his agent looking for help. Should the agent get a spec script for that new series that conforms to the head writer's vision, he'll surely share it with his client, the aforementioned frantic head writer. Speed is of the essence here."

Competition for TV writing gigs is fierce, the pace is grueling, and the culture takes some getting used to. But if you thrive on pressure and love the creative exchange of collaboration, TV might be your medium.

Learn more: "Screenplay, Writing the Picture" by Robin U. Russin and William Missouri Downs
http://www.tvwriter.com

88| US Copyright Office And The WGA

Registering with the US Copyright Office and the WGA doesn't give a writer any rights. It only proves he's claiming ownership. Nevertheless, there are advantages to registration as well as some differences between the two offices. Entertainment lawyer Judith Merians explains:

"The US Copyright Office: Registering a script with the US Copyright Office means the registrant is claiming to be the copyright owner and can sue another for copyright violation," says Merians. "Without a registration, there can be no suit. With registration, any proven claimant is entitled to a statutory $50,000 award, and any other damages proven in a copyright violation suit. US Copyright Office records are open to the public. Anyone can ask for a report on a project through a company like Thomson and Thomson.

"Under US law the laws of other countries who have copyright treaties with the US, any buyer of rights in intellectual property is responsible for knowing what is in the US Copyright Office records whether or not the buyer actually has that knowledge or not. Say Joe Green registers his claim as the copyright owner of his script in the US Copyright Office. Subsequently Big Bux Company buys Joe's script from Jane Brown, a fraudulent seller who put her name on it. Big Bux failed to order a copyright report when purchasing from Jane. Joe files a claim against Big Bux for copyright violation. Big Bux cannot successfully mount a defense stating it didn't know about Joe's copyright claim. The courts will rule that because Joe's claim was available in the public records, Bug Bux had 'apparent knowledge.'"

"A writer will be asked for chain of title showing legal ownership when selling a script. Many buyers ask for or order a copyright report. If the writer's name appears in US Copyright Office records as the sole claimant of ownership interest, that is considered a clear chain of title. A production company's attorney is required to have done due diligence and found a clear chain of title to the script before Errors and Omissions insurance can be issued."

The Writer's Guild of America (WGA) is a labor union for film, television, and other media writers. The Guild's primary function is to protect members' financial and creative rights by enforcing contracts, setting minimum payment rates, determining writing credits, and monitoring and collecting residuals. More information can be found at http://www.wga.org.

"Registering your script with the WGA gets you a date-stamped card with your filing number, the date of filing, and the name of your script and the writer," says Merians. "This is merely evidence that you were in possession of that script on that date. The WGA registration can be presented as evidence in a dispute, but the writer will still have to prove his ownership claim."

Registration is inexpensive. To be safe, register with both the US Copyright Office and the WGA. Membership is not required to register with the WGA.

The Working Writer

89| Stay Balanced

It takes an obsessive, stubborn personality to make it as a screenwriter, but it's important to remember there's more to life than movies. Certainly there's more to your life than screenwriting. Sure, you have to isolate yourself to get your work done, and yes, I understand you're on deadline and Christmas isn't happening this year. But if you systematically neglect other aspects of your life to chase a "written by" credit, you may live to regret it. Stay connected with family and friends, and use the social time away from writing to rest and re-arm your writerly mind. Pursue varied interests, hobbies, and sports. Develop a flexible life rhythm, working harder on some days and easing off now and then. Take care of yourself by eating well and exercising regularly. Allowing yourself to recharge and refresh your perspective will go a long way toward keeping you level-headed, happy, and balanced as you navigate the shark-infested waters of Hollywood. After all, you'll need your stamina and strength. And getting out and living it up will give you new material to write about. (Ha, and you thought you weren't working!)

90| Learn The Business

It's time to switch roles from writer to business person and educate yourself about who's who and what's what in Hollywood. Learning about the industry should be an ongoing process for all writers. Here are a few tips to get you started:

• Read the trades (Variety, Hollywood Reporter)

• Keep track of fellow screenwriters. Subscribe to magazines like Written By and Creative Screenwriting.

• Surf the Web. Visit the home pages of your favorite movies.

• Watch television programs like E! and others that cover show business

• Learn the names of the major players—heads of studios, influential agents, and other powerbrokers.

• Look up movies you love on IMDB and find out who produced them.

• Learn who just sold what to whom through subscription services like Done Deal Pro (http://www.donedealpro).

• Read screenwriting blogs.

• Get a job in the industry, even an entry-level position.

• If you live in L.A., get out and socialize. Go to screenings, workshops, coffee houses, and parties.

91| Behave Like A Professional

We writers are an odd lot. We spend most of our time hunched behind a computer screen, tapping away 'til the wee hours, fueled on caffeine and talking to ourselves. Is it any wonder we lose some of our social graces? As comfy as those week-old pajamas are, sooner or later you'll have to bathe, cut your fingernails, and face human beings. You'll want them thinking you're a professional. Here are some guidelines to follow:

Be courteous to everyone you meet. Never talk down to an assistant, snap at a reader, or belittle a hat-check girl. Besides being good manners, it's also good business sense. You never know where that person will end up in a year from now. Hat-check girl today, movie mogul tomorrow. Hey, it could happen. So spread good karma. Be nice.

Show backbone. Being courteous doesn't mean being subservient. Confidence and self-possession are charismatic qualities. People will respect you if you can express your opinion with assurance. So go ahead and speak your mind, politely and respectfully. And show even more confidence by keeping an open mind and listening to others.

Be easy to work with. Hollywood may be full of divas, but nobody really likes them. If you're a mega-star, guaranteed box-office hit, you may be able to get away with it—for a while. But as a novice writer, forget it. Leave your high horse in the stable.

Separate the professional from the personal. As a screenwriter, you'll be praised, rejected, replaced, rewritten, fired, and re-hired. Your script will be lauded, altered, butchered, crucified, and scrapped. It's just the way it goes. Don't take it personally.

Value and nurture your reputation. Write amazing scripts. Be reliable. Deliver on time. Communicate when you have a problem. Be supportive of other people, rival writers included. Refrain from gossip. Give credit where credit is due. Create miracles.

92| The Long Haul

To the blissfully unaware, being a screenwriter has a wonderfully glamorous ring to it. No boss, no schedule. Parties with moguls and stars. And just think of the money you can make once you sell that script!

Of course, you know better. You know the average overnight success takes 10 years to happen. You're willing to pay your dues and you're not about to jeopardize your future by marketing an unfinished and unprofessional script. You love to write, and you especially love the entire universe of screenplay craft, from the wonders of the three-act structure down to the nitty-gritty of formatting. You're committed and persistent. You're willing to work day and night if necessary, willing to sacrifice things other people take for granted—weekends, sleep—for your career. No wanna-be, you're in it for the long haul. You're the bona fide, genuine, real deal. Right?

93| Six Degrees Of Separation

Making it in Hollywood takes talent and skill. Without connections in the industry, though, you stand little chance of success, however brilliant your work may be. Unfortunately, you don't have connections. Or so you believe. A popular theory states any two people can be linked to each other through at most six other people. It's called six degrees of separation. If you don't have any connections to a Hollywood player, you probably know someone who knows someone who does.

Sit down and make a list of everyone you can think of with even a remote connection to the film industry. If you can't think of anyone, start with a list of everyone you know, period. Then contact everyone on that list. Tell them you'd like to learn more about the film industry, and ask them if they know anyone you can talk to.

Approach this exercise in the spirit of educating yourself about the business, and you'll be surprised how willing people are to help you. Whatever you do, never be pushy, desperate, or rude. If someone is unwilling to make a connection for you, let it go. If you force them to give you a name, they'll probably warn that person about you. If you back off, they'll remember you as a class act. The next time you ask for their help, they just might say yes.

94| Building Relationships

Once you've made contact with an industry pro, it's time to start building a relationship.

The best relationships happen naturally. It's the difference between a blind date where the partners are comparing each other against a list of criteria, and a more relaxed evening out with someone whose company you truly enjoy. The first is a forced and artificial situation. Each partner is only focused on what they think they want and need from the other person, and that only causes stress. The second is more natural. The partners are open to learning about each other. This allows space for a true relationship to develop.

A friend of mine is one of the smoothest networkers I know. Her secret? She's truly interested in other people. When she asks about someone's projects or interests, people sense her sincerity and enjoy talking to her. She's also a confident professional, and she speaks charmingly and passionately about her own projects. She approaches everyone in the spirit of exchange, and she's never pushy or aggressive. As a result, she's very well-connected and well-respected.

Most of us don't have her natural ability for flawlessly balancing business and pleasure. We end up coming across as too shy, too aggressive, or too desperate. Find a person whose people skills you admire. Go with her to a couple of events and see if you can pick up any pointers. In the meantime, here are a few tips to get you started:

Nobody likes to be bombarded, especially in a social situation. Let a relationship develop and the business will follow naturally. "Don't overwhelm producers with your scripts and ideas. Stay calm," says screenwriter Andrew Bennett. "Wait for them to ask what you're working on. That's your cue to segue into your pitch."

Show interest in others. Ask them about their projects—and pay attention when they talk! Never make someone feel like there are more interesting people in the room to talk to. Even if there are.

Invite a pro to lunch. Keep it friendly. Tell them you respect their expertise, and you'd like to learn more about the business. Approach people the right way, and you'll find they're quite willing to share their experience with you—especially if you're picking up the tab.

Whenever you make a good contact, stay in touch. Send a congratulatory note when their newest movie opens or an update with your latest contest win. Be judicious, however. Don't spam people on a regular basis.

Let people get to know the real you. After all, it's your unique point of view you're trying to sell, isn't it?

95| Networking And The Internet

Use the Internet to meet like-minded people, develop your craft, and learn from the pros. Join networking rings like http://www.TribeHollywood.com, or build a page at http://www.MyCreativeCommunity.com or http://www.MySpace.com. Do a Google search for screenwriting forums, blogs, and critique groups. Or create your own Web site and encourage people to come to you. Two warnings:

• Don't believe everything you read on the Internet. Scams abound. There are lots of unscrupulous people out there claiming to be agents or running contests but who are only interested in taking your money. Do your homework, and use your judgment. If something sounds too good to be true, it probably is. Walk away.

• Be careful not to spend more time surfing than writing. As wonderful a resource as the Internet is, nothing will do more for your career than putting your butt in that chair and writing, writing, writing. The next time you're taking a stroll through cyberspace, stop by my Web site, http://www.TheThirdDraft.com, and say hello. I'd love to hear from you!

The Writer's Life

96| The Writerly Attitude

Here's one from guest tipster Pedro de Alcantara: "To be a writer is a 24/7 occupation, although writing itself takes only a fraction of your day. Being a writer doesn't really mean to write for a living, or even to write at all, but to think as a writer, to see the world as a writer, to be in the world as a writer—in short, to have a writerly attitude. It means to love words; to see every human being, man, woman, and child as a character in a drama, unfolding in front of your eyes on an infinite stage; to sense people's motivations, their personal narratives, their back stories; to sense everyone's character arc, friends', colleagues', strangers'; to sense foretelling in a gesture, a word, an action; to sense dramatic tension and relaxation in the unfolding of an event; to sense myth and stereotype and archetype in people and in their interactions; to love analysis, synthesis, description, explanation, condensation, to understand that words can do anything and everything you want them to do.

"For a writer, to watch a Simpsons rerun is to study the three-act structure, the interweaving of plot and subplot, the unfolding of story as conflict. Every character in The Simpsons has an antagonist. Even Maggie: hers is the Baby With One Eyebrow. The writer wants to re-write all that falls under his eyes—cereal boxes, street signs, slogans, even medicine labels. The writer never stops being a writer: at night, he dreams of Jungian archetypes, Freudian erotica, and plain old horror movies. "The writerly attitude is a precondition to all writing, and the serious writer is forever sharpening it. Read, eavesdrop, spy. Become a psychologist, historian, and philosopher rolled into one. Travel to experience other cultures and their differing sense of the human theater. When the writerly attitude is in place, the pages will flow out of you like maple syrup out of Vermont."

97| Making Time To Write

The path from wanting to write to having written is in the writing. It's not in the dreaming, the planning, or the research. Writers write, it's as simple as that.

Some people write every day, others don't. I write in bursts. I work as a freelancer, and both my personality and my professional life demand alternation. Once I accepted this, I was able to find a rhythm that works for me. Deadlines help. When I know I'm entering a phase where other obligations will demand a great deal of my attention, I enroll in a writing class just to have a deadline. My husband, who's also a freelancer, writes new materials daily. He keeps a log and won't go to bed until he can make a note in it for that day. While I admire his disciplined style, I have my own way of doing things. He is he, and I am I.

First, determine what writing rhythms work best for you. Try writing every day. Try writing twice a week or only on the weekends. Try time limits and page limits. Try early mornings, try after midnight. Once you've discovered your preferences, be ruthless about protecting your writing time. Schedule it like any other important appointment, and then keep it.

Do whatever it takes. Close your door, disconnect your phone, ask someone to mind the kids. But sit down at the scheduled time until you complete what you said you would. Just you and the blank page. Without distractions.

Write even if you can't think of anything to write about. The biggest mistake you can make is to wait for inspiration. In what other line do you have the luxury of waiting until you feel like it to get busy? Whoever asked a heart surgeon if he felt like doing a triple bypass, or an airline pilot if he was in the mood to fly to Cincinnati? What if your waitress didn't bring you your food because she was waiting for inspiration?

Just write, whether you feel like it or not. If you're lucky, your fingers will fly across the keyboard effortlessly. If you're not, the session must take place all the same. Heart surgery involves blood. Waitressing involves sore feet. Writing involves producing pages. That's just the way it is. Love it or hate it, that's what a writer does.

98| A Space For Your Writing

Besides establishing a rhythm for your writing, carve out a special space for it, too. Whether you turn a spare bedroom into a writer's den or stow your stuff in the glove compartment and write on the dashboard of your car is up to you. The important thing is for you to associate some little corner of the universe with the act of writing. Create a place you like being in. Fill it with things that inspire you. Strip it of every distraction. Make it yours.

I have different spaces for different parts of the writing process. I brainstorm in an armchair in the corner of my office, but I compose at my desk. When I had a larger kitchen, I loved working at the kitchen table. I generally prefer to work from home, but sometimes I go to a café especially when I'm proofreading or editing. I have a harder time with other public places, though I have done good work in planes, trains, and hotel rooms.

Sometimes, just by shifting locations you can get the creative juices flowing. Try out different spots until you figure out what combination works best for you.

99| Tools Of The Trade

All anyone really needs to jot down his thoughts is a stick and some dirt, but it's hard to develop a fetish for mud. How lucky we are, then, that humanity invented office supplies. Oh, how much time we can waste searching for that elusive, perfect blank notebook! Not too fat. Not too thin. With just the right feel. And just the right scent. Procrastination never smelled so good.

Well, indulge yourself from time to time. Choosing, collecting, and readying your writing tools can be an integral part of the preparation. For me, picking up paper and pencil signals my mind that I'm ready for brainstorming. Sitting at the computer sends a message that it's time for lucidity. Grabbing a fountain pen and my journal means I'm about to get personal.

The right tools can focus you for the job ahead, whatever that may be. The danger lies in believing you can't write without the proper tools, which isn't true, of course. A real writer can make do with whatever is at hand, including mud. But if you have a choice, why not use whatever speaks to you most?

100| Learn From Rejection

Rejection has happened to every writer, director, producer, actor, and actress in the business. Even successful writers and famous stars are sometimes rejected. J.K. Rowling's baby was turned down by many publishers before becoming *Harry Potter*. What makes you think it won't happen to you?

To submit means running the risk of rejection. Until you run that risk, you won't have a shot at success. The sooner you accept rejection as an unavoidable part of the process, the better.

The good news is that you get to choose how you react to rejection. You can either become depressed and discouraged, or you can decide to learn from rejection. As Hamlet famously said, "There is nothing either good or bad but thinking makes it so."

Like all writers, Pedro de Alcantara has faced his share of rejection. Below, he shares some of the reactions to rejection he has personally experienced. A few, he admits, are more constructive than others:

· Rejected again! I'm no good. I'll never succeed.

· Rejection? So be it. Tonight I'll give myself a little treat for comfort—sushi and sake, or maybe a stop at the jazz club—and tomorrow is another day.

· Well, the feedback was harsher than necessary, but the reader had a few good points. After I stop hating him I'm going to try another draft.

· This project is good, really good. I haven't found the right production company for it yet, though. I'll have to keep trying.

With time, de Alcantara has learned to optimize the rejection experience:

· A little distance, a little time, a little laughter are all helpful in dealing with most problems.

· In every community there are people who quite enjoy the company of embittered cynics. But you might stand a better chance of success if you're reasonable, attentive, open-minded, and generous to everyone, including people who have rejected your work.

· Keep track of your rejections, as you would of your submissions. First, you don't want to submit the same project to the same people twice. Second, start discerning patterns of feedback. Collective wisdom is usually right. If five producers all make similar points, you might want to listen.

101| Start Your Next Script: When More Is More

Some novice writers get stuck in writing, re-writing, polishing, and marketing their one and only script for years, a surefire recipe for frustration and disaster. They'd have better chances of sparking their creativity, boosting their output, and furthering their careers if they gave that script a break and started a new project.

"This business isn't about one project. It's about consistently returning to your contacts with the next great movie," says producer Hal Croasmun. "Do that and you'll build a career."

Writer Pedro de Alcantara gives us these tips for working on more than one project at a time:

Take a seasoned screenwriter you admire, and make a list of his finished projects. Let's consider Richard Brooks (Elmer Gantry, 1960; Lord Jim, 1965; Looking for Mr. Goodbar, 1977). His career spanned more than forty years and boasted several dozen finished projects, including several novels. Now imagine you're 80 years old and, like Brooks, you too have dozens of films to your credit. How will you have accomplished all of that?

Realize you need to juggle several projects at the same time. You won't fulfill your talents—or earn a decent living—if you work on a single project alone, from beginning to end, before taking on another one. The endless rounds of drafts, the possibility of rejection, the time spent in development hell could mean each project will face a 10-year slog with an uncertain outcome. That's just not fun.

Alternate between projects, and vary the level of commitment to each one. If you're under a tight deadline, that project ought to take precedence. But there's a lot of merit in your preparing, sketching, or simply "dreaming" another project at the same time. Take breaks from working on the main project and do a little research on the secondary one. Two hours one afternoon, a few moments Googling this or that another time. Breaks allow the main project to "rest" while another one "works." Before you know it, you'll have a new script shaping up even as you put the finishing touches on that urgent project.

Accept that the screenwriter's life includes many activities: reading, researching, outlining, drafting, revising, taking meetings, networking, attending screenings, and more. Working on any one project demands a variety of skills and the ability to do many things at the same time. If you already need to do six or eight things for your current project, it isn't that hard to do another one or two on another project.

Find the right number of activities for your temperament. Give each activity its proper weight, and find a fluid rhythm for alternating activities. You may discover that the best rhythm and the best alternation may well require a greater number of activities than you thought

List of Resources

Websites:

Done Deal Pro
http://www.donedealpro.com
This site tracks script and pitch sales and options, and offers a searchable database (subscribers only).

Internet Movie Database (IMDB)
http://www.imdb.com
A database of movies and credits.

Movie Bytes
http://www.moviebytes.com
A listing of screenwriting contests and markets.

Script for Sale
http://www.scriptforsale.com
Producer Hal Croasmun's site. Articles, tools, classes, and a free newsletter.

Classes:

UCLA Extension Courses. Take them in person if you're in L.A., or online: http://www.uclaextension.edu

Gotham Writer's Workshop for live classes in New York, or study online: http://www.writingclasses.com

One **free option** for beginners is http://www.freefilmschool.org.

If you're looking for a **degree program**, here's a listing of film programs in the US and abroad:
http://www.filmmaking.net/directory/filmschools

Screenwriting Books:

Alternative Scriptwriting by Ken Dancyger & Jeff Rush

Breakfast with Sharks, by Michael Lent

Global Scriptwriting by Ken Dancyger

Making a Good Script Great and *Advanced Screenwriting* by Linda Seger

Save the Cat, by Blake Snyder

Screenplay, Writing the Picture by Robin U. Russin and William Missouri Downs

Story: Substance, Structure, Style and The Principles of Screenwriting, by Robert McKee

The Savvy Screenwriter, by Susan Kouguell

The Writer's Journey: Mythic Structure for Writers, by Christopher Vogler

Writing for Emotional Impact and *101 Habits of Highly Successful Screenwriters*, by Karl Iglesias

Magazines and Publications:

Creative Screenwriting Magazine:
http://www.creativescreenwriting.com

Filmmaker: http://www.filmmakermagazine.com

The Hollywood Reporter: http://hollywoodreporter.com

Variety : http://www.variety.com/

Written By. http://www.wga.org/writtenby/writtenby.aspx

Screenwriting Software:

Final Draft and **Movie Magic** are the two pre-eminent formatting programs.

For more details on these and other programs, go to:
http://dvshop.ca/dvcafe/writing/formatting.html

Directories:

Hollywood Creative Directory for listings of producers and executives, and the *Hollywood Representation Directory* for listings of agents. Invaluable. Published several times a year.
http://www.hcdonline.com

More Titles in the LifeTips Book Series

101 Plus Size Women's Clothing Tips
by Lynda Moultry

101 Marathon Tips
by Heidi Splete

101 Autism Tips
by Tammi Reynolds

CPSIA information can be obtained
at www.ICGtesting.com
Printed in the USA
LVHW081249081119
636774LV00015B/233/P

9 781602 750159